THE JEWISH FARMERS OF WESTERN CANADA

By Cyril Edel Leonoff

Part I: Beginnings of Land Settlement

Jewish land settlement in Western Canada had its origin in 1881 in the Empire of Russia when revolutionaries assassinated Czar Alexander II. Confusion reigned throughout the country, and the reactionary government used the Jews as scapegoats, encouraging the illusion that through control of commerce, industry and much land they were responsible for the misfortunes of the nation.

While the Jewish position in Russian society had heretofore been tenuous, this was the first time that large-scale physical attacks (pogroms) broke out in a number of locales in Southern Russia. In May, 1882 the Czarist regime promulgated the infamous "May Laws," which expelled Jews from all hamlets and villages, and prohibited purchase or rental of land by Jews for agricultural purposes.[1] The riots continued through 1883, rendering 100,000 Jews homeless and property damage estimated at $80 million.[2] Finding their situation hopeless, Russian Jews started a large-scale emigration.

Some gravitated to the ancestral homeland of Palestine, participating in the first *aliyah* to the Holy Land. This Hibbat Zion (Love of Zion) movement resulted in the founding of early agricultural colonies in Israel. Others looked westward towards the land that was broadly known to them as "America," where they heard there was freedom from oppression and opportunity for land settlement was available to all newcomers.

Protest meetings against harsh Russian actions were held in principal cities throughout the world. Faced with growing numbers of Russian-Jewish refugees in the impoverished East End of London, in February, 1882 a protest meeting was held in Mansion House Hall, presided over by the Lord Mayor and other dignitaries. Out of this meeting a Russo-Jewish Committee was formed

---

1. *Encyclopedia* Judaica, Vol. 14, pp. 444-446, Vol. 11, pp. 1147-1148.
2. Simon Belkin, *Through Narrow Gates* (Montreal, 1966), p. 27, quoting Mark Wischnitzer, *Visas to Freedom*, p. 29.

and a fund established to assist in resettling the displaced people. Attending the meeting was Sir Alexander T. Galt, the Canadian High Commissioner in London. Galt was responsible for implementing Canada's national policy of economic growth by attracting potential settlers to Western Canada where, in 1882, vast agricultural lands were being opened up through construction of the Canadian Pacific Railway (CPR) across the prairies. In this pursuit, Galt became a trustee of the Russo-Jewish Committee.[3] While preference was given to emigrants from the British Isles and Western Europe, in a series of letters Galt persuaded the skeptical Prime Minister of Canada, Sir John A. Macdonald, to accept a number of Russian-Jewish refugees.[4]

In May and June, 1882, 340 Jewish immigrants arrived at Winnipeg, Manitoba, the "Gateway to the West." The existing Jewish community which in 1881 comprised thirty-three families, found it difficult to absorb a group much larger than itself.[5] Following the advice of Galt, the objective of the Russo-Jewish Committee was "to combine the plight of these unfortunate Jews with a practical plan of assistance and thus make them economically independent individuals upon the soil of a new and free land."[6] However, owing to lack of suitable preparation by the committee and failure of the government to assign a tract of land, it took two full years for the refugees to set up their own group farm colony in the Canadian Northwest. The hope was that this would be the nucleus of several Jewish colonies proposed for Western Canada.

Owing to the efforts of Galt, by mid-May, 1884, land was finally occupied twenty-five miles southwest of the railway connection at Moosomin, in what was then known as the Assiniboia District of the North-West Territories, but now is in the Province of Saskatchewan. The novelty of Jewish farmers evoked considerable curiosity in the district and the Moosomin colony became

---

3. Belkin, pp. 28-29; Arthur A. Chiel, *The Jews in Manitoba* (Toronto, 1961), pp. 26-29.
4. Public Archives of Canada (PAC), MG 26 A, vol. 219, Galt to Macdonald: Jan. 25, 1882, pp. 93321-22; Jan. 28, 1882, pp. 93323-24; March 22, 1882, pp. 93409-10; April 5, 1882, pp. 93431-32; Feb. 3, 1882, pp. 93327-28; July 7, 1882, p. 93533; July 8, 1883, p. 93543; Joseph Pope, *Selections from Macdonald Correspondence*, Macdonld to Galt, Feb. 26, 1882, p. 286, PAC, MG 26 A 1 (e), vol. 574 LB 21, Macdonald to Galt, Feb. 27, 1882, pp. 680-681.
5. Chiel, pp. 29-33.
6. Arthur D. Hart, ed., *The Jew in Canada* (Toronto and Montreal, 1926), p. 62.

known under the nickname "New Jerusalem." While Galt had initially intended to settle forty to fifty farmers, only twenty-seven families took advantage of the opportunity, the others in the meantime having found work in railway construction or in other occupations.

Within a forty-eight-mile belt bordering the railway, the CPR had been granted an equal number of sections (odd-numbered) with the government (even-numbered). Only the government sections were available to the settlers on the homestead plan. Under the Dominion Lands Act of 1872, the government provided a free

John Heppner homestead, established in 1886 near
Wapella, Saskatchewan, the first permanent Jewish farm in Canada.

homestead of a quarter section (160 acres) at a nominal registration fee of ten dollars. Before a homesteader would be granted title he had to have been in residence for three years, erected a habitable home, and cultivated a reasonable portion of the land. The homesteader was also given a preemption to purchase an adjoining quarter section at a price of one dollar per acre.

The tract occupied by the Jewish farmers was 8,968 acres divided into quarter sections. They took up twenty-seven homestead quarters and twenty-four preemptions. The Mansion House Fund extended a total of $15,000, with each farmer receiving loans from $259 to a maximum of $485. This assistance was inadequate and moreover, none of the settlers were conditioned to pioneering life and none had experience in Canadian farming.

From the outset "New Jerusalem" was beset with the problems that plagued many early agricultural attempts in the northwest prairies. These included early frost in the fall of 1884; inadequate winter shelter against the sub-zero temperatures, winds and driving snow; destruction of the crops by hail and an early frost in August, 1885; and general drought in the region in 1886.[7] By the winter of 1885-1886 some socio-cultural gains were made, including a small synagogue and Hebrew school, but the benefits of these were lost in December, 1886 when the rabbi-teacher of the community was caught in a blizzard and had his feet so badly frozen that they had to be amputated.[8]

By 1888 Galt bitterly declared the Jewish colony a failure and denounced his proteges as "vagabonds" who he stated "had turned to their natural avocation for peddling."[9] After several years of unrelenting struggle, the final disaster struck in September, 1889 when fire destroyed the entire hay crop. The colonists suspected arson and were dissatisfied with the police investigation. In April, 1890 a local paper reported that "A number of . . . families from the Jew colony . . . passed on their way to Winnipeg. The settlement will soon be depopulated."[10] Several of these so-called "vagabonds" settled permanently in Winnipeg where they became successful businessmen and were among the founders of one of the most culturally vibrant Jewish communities in North America.

While "New Jerusalem" was floundering another small experiment was underway which was to make a larger contribution to Jewish land settlement in Western Canada. The instigator was Hermann Landau, a prominent Anglo-Jewish financier, and representative of the CPR in London. He had been born in Russian-

---

7. The Moosomin colony is treated fully in Belkin, pp. 56-57, 212; Chiel, pp. 44-47; Bob Irving and Maxine Povering, "Jewish Agricultural Colonization in Canada: The Moosomin Experiment," Dissertation, University of Waterloo, 1980, 33 pp. with maps.
8. *Moosomin Courier*, December 9, 16, 1886.
9. PAC, RG 15, vol. 318, file 73568 (1), Galt, Montreal, to A. M. Burgess, Secretary, Commission of Dominion Lands, Winnipeg, January 30, 1888.
10. *Fairmede News*, April 16, 1890.

Poland in 1844. After receiving an Orthodox Jewish education in Breslau (now Wroclaw, Poland), he emigrated to England where he became a teacher of Hebrew in Dover in 1864. In 1866 he moved to Brighton to study law, but abandoned the profession after realizing that one needed influence to succeed at the Bar. Landau rebeled against the exclusive rights held by English-born Jews in the management of Jewish communal affairs. He success-

Abraham Klenman, patriarch of the Wapella colony, 1888-1910.

fully championed the rights of the foreign-born Jew as "the social and intellectual equal of the native English Jew." In 1871 Landau settled in London and entered the Stock Exchange, where he soon won a fortune. Enjoying his wealth, time and energy, Landau became staunchly supportive of those Anglo-Jewish institutions devoted to the social and economic betterment of his foreign-born brethren in the East End of London. In the course of his financial career he became interested in foreign projects in developing regions of the British Empire. He dreamed of a broad colonization scheme for the East European Jewish refugees.[11] To Hermann Landau the Canadian West seemed an ideal land for resettlement. His study of the Canadian potential is evident in a lecture which he later delivered before a Jewish literary society in London:

> With the opening of Canada by means of the Canadian Pacific Railway, the natural resources . . . 5,000,000 acres . . . of wheat land . . . began to be developed. The Grand Trunk Pacific [Railway], which was now in the course of construction, would in a few years lay open no less than 300,000,000 acres of land which would grow wheat . . . without artificial aid. . . .
>
> [I] had for many years . . . since 1882, strongly advocated the concentration of all Russo-Jewish refugees . . . in Canada, where the climate was similar to the one they were born under, and where religious tolerance had become the religion of the country — if [I] might so term it. There was no sect that had not found the same rights under the broad and hospitable constitution of the Dominion of Canada.[12]

In this address Landau related his contribution to a successful case history of the Jewish farming experience in Canada:

> [I] had some experience of founding a small colony in 1885 at a place called Wapella, [228] miles west of Winnipeg. After the May Laws were enacted . . . a very large number of Russian Jews migrated to England, the United States, Canada, and other places. The then Russo-Jewish Committee selected at the [London] Shelter twelve young men with a view to having them put upon farms at Aylesbury [England] where, after a year, they became excellent farm hands.

Impatient with the slow progress of the Russo-Jewish Committee, and acting on his own, Landau had selected eleven persons comprising the John Heppner family of two men and three women, and six single men from the Aylesbury group, by now somewhat conversant in English and familiar with farming, and sent them to Canada. In 1906 Landau could proudly report that "The colonists there were not only doing well, but were becoming prosperous men."[13]

On September 2, 1886 Alexander Begg, CPR Emigrations

---

11. Arthur A. Chiel, "Hermann Landau's Canadian Dream," *Canadian Jewish Historical Society Journal*, Fall 1978, pp. 113-120; "Death of Mr. Hermann Landau, O.B.E., *The Jewish Chronicle*, London, September 2, 1921, pp. 19-20.
12. "Mr. Hermann Landau on Canada and the Jews," *Ibid.*, January 19, 1906. p. 16.
13. *Ibid.*

Agent in London, wrote to the Land Commissioner of the company in Winnipeg that "a party of Russian Jews sail from here . . . today . . . sent out by Mr. Landau, one of our biggest financiers." They are "a superior class" from those already settled near Moosomin and "thorough agriculturists." If these people are comfortably settled in the Northwest, and send home good reports, "the result will be a very large emigration of people from Russia of the bet-

Edel Brotman, farmer-rabbi of the Wapella colony, 1889-1906.

ter class, having from 500 to 1,000 pounds capital per family."[14] The sad reputation of the settlers at "New Jerusalem" had reached London, so Begg continued his advice to the commissioner that Landau "would have no objection to their being settled on homesteads near the colony of Moosomin . . . if their knowledge of farming and frugal, temperate and cleanly ways would tend to elevate the people now settled at Moosomin." But in no case would he run the risk of "contamination" of his own people. Begg's idea,

14. PAC, Dominion Lands Bureau, Record Group 15, Series B-1a, vol. 122, file 128731, Alex. Begg, CPR to J. H. McTavish, CPR, copy to Dept. of the Interior, Ottawa.

however, was that these people should be settled "by themselves in some good locality," and advised that they could take up eight homesteads in a party. All that was necessary to accommodate the Heppner family and the six men would be to build a couple of houses "as inexpensive as possible, just sufficient to keep them warm, and comfortable for the winter." He further instructed the commissioner that they could go right on with farming operations in the spring "if you could manage to get a few acres of land broken for them this fall." In the matter of finances Begg said that in addition to what money the Heppners have themselves, as a start off "Mr. Landau authorizes us to spend 50 pounds. The others of the party will have about 400 pounds between them . . . so it seems to me you will be able to manage with this." Begg made it plain that the funds advanced were not an outright grant as "Mr. Landau will wish to have security on the homesteads."[15]

The sums stated by Begg were either inaccurate or inadequate. Later, a claim in the amount of $2,509.47 against the eleven Russian Jews was made to the Minister of the Interior under the Dominion Lands Act. The claim stated, "as they had no money," Mr. J. H. McTavish, Land Commissioner of the CPR, "advanced them money . . . to go to Wapella in the North-West Territories," and has since then "from time to time made advances . . . for the purpose of buying stock and provisions." He "settled them all on homestead lands north of Wapella, and they are now farming there."[16] The minister approved the claim and apparently the liens were taken.[17]

On September 20, 1886 H. H. Smith, Commissioner of Dominion Lands in Winnipeg, reported to the minister that he had, at Mr. McTavish' request, telegraphed instructions to the local agent to reserve any vacant lands in Townships 15 and 16. Ranges 32 and 33 west of the First Meridian "from which . . . the Russians will be able to make selections [of eight homesteads] to their satisfaction."[18] The land selected was six miles northeast of the

15. *Ibid.*
16. *Ibid.*, Macdonald. Tupper & Phippen, Attorneys, Winnipeg to Minister of the Interior, Ottawa, December 29, 1887.
17. *Ibid.*, P. C. Douglas. Asst. Secretary, Interior, Ottawa to Macdonald, Tupper, etc., January 24, 1888.
18. *Ibid.*, H. H. Smith to Hon. Thomas White, Minister Interior.

CPR mainline at Wapella in what is now the Rocanville District of Saskatchewan. Though only thirty miles northeast of "New Jerusalem," the new settlement was far enough away so that, insofar as is known, the two colonies never had contact.

Wapella homestead of Kalman Isman family, built 1889. It is a typical pioneer log house, mud-plastered and whitewashed. The original sod roof was replaced with shingles. This family and its descendants have tilled the soil of Saskatchewan for 95 years.

On March 24, 1887 McTavish was able to report that "I found a very fine tract of country, on which there were not many settlers," in Township 16.32. W1, and "I purchased a homestead from a settler who had been there some time with considerable breaking done and a good house on it . . . which would be a sort of headquarters for the people . . . during the winter . . . while they are getting ready to go on their homesteads." McTavish went on to relate a very unusual concession made to the Jewish settlers. "These eight men wished particularly to be together, so as to form a sort of nucleus for a large number of their coreligionists whom they expected out in the event of their venture proving successful, and the only way I could so locate them was to let them have odd

9

sections . . . adjoining the even ones, the CPR receiving vacant even quarter-sections from the Government in lieu thereof."[19] The Minister of the Interior approved and instructed the local agent "to effect these exchanges without payment of additional fees."[20]

However, the cordiality bestowed upon the Russian Jews by the CPR and the government officials, unfortunately, was not extended by the local residents.

> At a general meeting of the Liberal Conservative Association, Wapella, April 18, 1887, it was resolved that . . . our honorable friends the Government are unaware of the injury done to us by reserving sections in . . . this district for the settlement of Jews. Not only are Jews a most undesirable class of settlers but they are keeping a number of desirable settlers out to our present and future detriment.

The resolution referred to "a number of well-to-do [English] farmers who will bring a considerable amount of capital with them and unless the reserved sections are thrown open these gentlemen will regretfully seek elsewhere . . . and doubtless that . . . will be Dakota."[21]

The resolution, signed by twenty-two members of the governing party, was transmitted to the Department of the Interior by W. D. Perley, the local member of Parliament, and could not be politically ignored.[22] The minister's office advised Perley that "before the minister can take any action" he would have to obtain a report on the situation. Therefore the Commissioner of Lands was instructed to dispatch a Homestead Inspector to "report fully as to the condition and character of these Jewish settlers, and the manner in which they are fulfilling their homestead duties."[23]

Before the minister's instructions were received, however, the Dominion Lands Commission office had acted precipitously only eight days after receiving the Wapella resolution, and reported to the department who informed Perley, "that the reservation of the lands in Townships 15 and 16 in Ranges 32 and 33 West . . . was

---

19. *Ibid.*, McTavish to Smith.
20. *Ibid.*, Douglas to Smith, September 4, 1887.
21. *Ibid.*, Resolution Liberal Conservative Association, Wapella.
22. *Ibid.*, A. M. Burgess, Deputy Minister, Ottawa, to W. D. Perley, Ottawa, May 3, 1887.
23. *Ibid.*, Burgess to Smith, May 3, 1887.

discontinued on the 26th April last.[24] There was another reserve (for Russian Jews) . . . in Townships 11, 12 and 13, Range 2 W. 2nd. M. ["New Jerusalem"] which has also been discontinued."[25]

On July 19, 1887 the inspector reported from Moosomin on the Heppner party in Township 16:

Hirsch Jacobson's log barn, Wapella colony. Note the mud-plastered wall reinforced with willow wattling, typical of prairie pioneer construction.

In answer as to their condition and prosperity, and whether they can be classed as good settlers likely to prove a benefit to the country, I have to say that the English settlers speak highly of these Jews, and don't desire better neighbors, that they are very industrious and hard working . . . and in every way, able to discharge their conditions of settlement. . . . A class of settlers such as these men are, cannot but be beneficient to the country.[26]

The positive report of the inspector allowed the exchange of sec-

---

24. *Ibid.*, F. B. Burpe, Secretary, Lands Commission, Winnipeg, to Secretary, Interior, Ottawa, June 7, 1887.

25. *Ibid.*, Douglas to Perley, House of Commons, June 14, 1887.

26. *Ibid.*, R. S. Park, Homestead Inspector, Moosomin, to Smith.

tions to proceed.[27] Nevertheless, cancellation of the reserves was not rescinded.[28]

The scheme originally envisioned by Landau was to match two of the young farmers to Heppner's "two beautiful daughters," but there was a scarcity of women and the girls found more prosperous suitors in Winnipeg.[29] Within a year, the six single men of Landau's "superior class," lacking womenfolk, had fled their homesteads never to be heard from again in Western Canada.

Surprisingly, the failures of "New Jerusalem" and the Landau-sponsored group did not end Jewish land settlement in the Moosomin-Wapella district. Another group, by their own initiative, unsupported by government or philanthropic agencies, but imbued with the Jewish back-to-the-land movement, were to open a new chapter. These people, who had some rudimentary farming experience in Russia, were to found the first successful Jewish farm settlement in Canada and thus dispelled the common belief that Jews made unsuccessful farmers. This small-scale settlement north of Wapella was the forerunner of some dozen Jewish farm colonies in Western Canada.

In 1888 Abraham Klenman of Soroki, Bessarabia, a border region between Russia and Roumania, arrived in Montreal with his family and son-in-law, Solomon Barish. Many of the Jews in Soroki engaged in agriculture, primarily in the growing of tobacco, grapes and other fruit.[30] Klenman had overseen an agricultural estate for an absentee Russian landlord, while Barish had farmed in the Jewish farm colony of Dombroveni, which had developed the most advanced level of farm economy in the Jewish colonies of that region.[31]

Their immediate problem in Montreal was to find work to support their families. So Barish started to peddle in a rural district. Speaking neither French nor English he was under a considerable handicap and soon gave up peddling to work in a cigar factory. Klenman, who was fifty-seven, was destined to realize his

27. *Ibid.*, Douglas to Smith and The Agent of Dominion Lands, Birtle, Manitoba, September 4, 1887.
28. *Ibid.*, Memorandum, Interior, to Deputy Minister, June 14, 1889.
29. *The Jewish Chronicle*, January 19, 1906, p. 16.
30. *Encyclopedia Judaica*, Vol. 15, p. 166.
31. *Ibid.*, Vol. 6, p. 157.

ambition that had motivated his emigration to Canada, and he re-
solved to go west and settle on a homestead. To Jews who had been
barred from owning land in the old country, the "free" land offered by the Canadian Government was inviting.

Klenman agitated among his Jewish immigrant compatriots,
with the result that by the fall of 1888 he and Jacob Silver were
appointed as a party of investigation to travel west and find a
suitable tract of land. Stopping off in Winnipeg they had a cordial
meeting with L. A. Hamilton, who on McTavish' death had succeeded him as Land Commissioner of the CPR. Hamilton sent the

The Barish farm, Wapella colony, developed out of the
original homestead, 1894-1958.

party to Deloraine, Manitoba in the company of an official who
could speak German, a tongue akin to the Yiddish spoken by
Klenman and Silver. They did not take up land in that district as
the soil was too light to attract farmers accustomed to the fertile
black soil of Bessarabia. They went farther west and were offered homesteads near the then village of Regina (now the capital
of Saskatchewan). Here again they were not attracted to the heavy
gumbo clay soil of that prairie plain, that was sticky in wet weather
and baked easily when dry. Having no money to buy lumber they
decided to settle in the aspen parkland belt which was covered by
trees and bushes in order to make use of the wood for buildings and
fuel. Also, they knew that in the bush country the necessary water

supply would be near the surface, while on the plain it was at a considerable depth. However, the area required exhausting labor to clear the land and root out the stumps by hand.

While in the neighborhood Klenman heard that another Jewish farmer, John Heppner, had settled near Wapella. By that time the Heppner family was the lone remnant of the Landau group. Klenman was naturally attracted by the presence of another Jewish farmer. Finding the land forested and having a fertile black loam soil, he decided to settle on land adjoining Heppner's farm. Jacob Silver returned to Montreal to report on the venture. However, Klenman took up his homestead and started to build a log house with a straw roof. He was accustomed in Southern Europe to a longer summer season. But the Canadian winter had set in by the time he had hand-dug a cellar. So he covered it with poles and put straw on the top, with a square hole in the roof and a ladder for entry. Klenman lived like a prairie gopher during that first winter in what was literally a hole in the ground. On completion of the house next spring his family came from Montreal.

Solomon Barish did not settle in Wapella immediately. Working in Montreal to support his wife and family, he sent them out ahead to live with Klenman. Then he trained for a year in Chicago to become a *schochet* and *mohel*, in order to serve the ritual needs not only of the Wapella colony but of the many scattered Jewish farmers and storekeepers who were then beginning to take up residence in the Canadian Northwest. In 1892 Barish arrived in Winnipeg with $100, which was sufficient to pay his fare out to the farm, and to buy a team of oxen, a plough and wagon in order to begin farming.[32]

In the spring of 1889 Klenman's followers made preparations to join him at Wapella. Again the Jewish settlers were helped by the CPR. On July 9, 1889 the Dominion Lands Commission secretary in Winnipeg advised the Department of the Interior in Ottawa, "Last spring Mr. Hamilton, of the CPR Co., reported to the commissioner that certain other Jews had or were about to arrive

---

32. Louis Rosenberg, "Wapella: The Oldest Existing Jewish Farm Colony in Canada," *The Jewish Post*, Winnipeg. Sept. 14, 1928, pp. 21-22; Cyril Edel Leonoff, "Wapella Farm Settlement: The First Successful Jewish Farm Settlement in Canada," *Manitoba Historical and Scientific Society Transactions*, Series III, No. 27, 1970-71, pp. 25-59.

and . . . it was desirable that they should be enabled to settle in the neighborhood of their compatriots."[33] Once more the minister received a petition from the Wapella Association:

> . . . we have all come here as independent settlers, pioneers as it were, for our friends and relatives whom we are hoping will join us in filling up this sparsely settled country.
>
> We humbly pray, and consider, that you should give us all the encouragement in your power . . . in making this a compact and prosperous district.
>
> Especially do we protest against the reservation of lands in our midst for the settlement of Jews.[34]

Since the hoped-for English settlers in any numbers still were not forthcoming to fill the vacant lands, the Jews already there were able to obtain their homesteads as individual settlers, but not as an organized ethnic colony. And through the interchange precedent already established, they were able to obtain adjoining homesteads.

Between the spring of 1889 and the fall of 1892 some twenty-eight Jewish families followed Klenman to the district. Most were recent immigrants at Montreal. A few had begun farming in North Dakota, and some had been construction workers on the railway. Most of the settlers were from Southern Russia and Bessarabia, with a sprinkling of Roumanian, Galician and Lithuanian Jews. Other than Klenman and Barish few had been farmers in the old country. One had run a tobacco plantation. Another was an expert horseman from the Russian army. The majority had been unskilled laborers and pedlars. Hirsch Jacobson exemplified the spirit and determination of the latter group.

> The reason I left my homeland at age twenty-one was that the Jewish people did not have the same rights as the Russians had. Their laws made me mad because the Jews were not allowed to occupy themselves at farming. They foolishly thought that a Jew did not have the ability to farm. Then I had to go into the army. So instead I thought it would be better to prove that a Jew could be a farmer as well as a Russian could.
>
> I realized my ambition in Wapella, Canada. I started alone and with no experience, uprooted trees, cleared brush, and

---

33. PAC, RG 15, B-1a, vol. 122, file 128731, Burpe to Secretary, Interior.
34. *Ibid.*, Petition, to Hon. Edgar Dewdney, Minister Interior, June 29, 1889.

broke up the land. Eventually with the help of my wife and son I became a "big" farmer, work three quarters of land, have lots of cattle and horses, and full equipment from a needle to a threshing machine. I have made the land one of the most fruitful farms in the district, and have proved that a Jew can be a farmer as well as anybody else.[35]

The lifestyle of the Wapella farmers, their hardships, and accomplishments have been documented in another study.[36] The Jewish community of Wapella was never large enough or sufficiently organized to maintain its own institutions other than religious services. They shared with the general population the facilities of schools, commercial and farm organizations, social and fraternal societies, and other facets of rural life. They thereby adapted to the new environment much more readily than a group set apart.

Being Orthodox Jews, there were a number of religious requirements to be fulfilled. A Wapella Hebrew Congregation was formed. In 1889 Edel Brotman and three sons took up homesteads. Brotman had studied in a yeshiva and qualified as a rabbi in his native Galicia. For sixteen years he acted as the rabbi of the settlement, performing religious services and marriages. Fluent in seven languages, he also became the local immigration agent. When Brotman departed, Solomon Barish or visiting religious men cared for the ritual needs of the community.

The private enterprise Jewish farmers of Wapella, starting without financial aid from government or philanthropic societies, exhibited a will to succeed in comparison with other colonies such as "New Jerusalem," and later Hirsch and Qu'Appelle, which often were bogged down in official red tape and seemed to lack individual initiative. Not until 1901, when their crops were destroyed by frost, did they receive outside assistance. Twenty-seven Wapella farmers obtained loans from The Jewish Agricultural Society of New York, which they repaid in full within seventeen years.[37]

---

35. Solomon Hirsch Jacobson, "Reminiscences of My Pioneer Days," address to The Prosperity Homemakers Club, Rocanville Munic., Sask., and Rosenberg, ed., *The Jewish Post, Nov. 30, 1937*, pp. 15-16.
36. Leonoff, "Wapella."
37. The Jewish Agricultural and Industrial Aid Society, *Annual Reports*, New York, 1902, p. 25, 1918, p. 44. This was a subsidiary of the Baron de Hirsch Fund.

Many of the English neighbors had reason to regret their initial presumptive evaluation of the Jews. Once they had proved themselves as good citizens and able farmers, the Jewish people were treated as equals. There were several instances of record where Jewish and English settlers, including even signers of the anti-Jewish resolutions, were neighbors and close friends on the Wapella farms for up to fifty years.

What is the validity of the claim to success of the Wapella Jewish colony? John Heppner retired by 1908 but his Canadian-born son Max carried on the farm and a grain business, reportedly becoming "one of the most prosperous Jewish farmers in Canada."[38] The principals of the Klenman group including Klenman, Barish and Jacobson, lived the remainder of their lives on the farms. And their descendants farmed for two generations or more. Most of Klenman's followers remained on their farms into the twentieth century. A few did not endure the hardships of pioneering homesteaders for long, and gravitated to the new towns and cities which were then springing up on the prairies, becoming successful tradesmen and merchants. The most famous of these was the Ekiel Bronfman family who later gained international prominence in business and finance.[39]

The dropout rate of the Jewish settlement at Wapella compared favorably with other contemporary ethnic colonies in the region. These included the well-financed English settlement at Cannington Manor, twenty miles south of "New Jerusalem;"[40] the settlement of French nobility at Whitewood, fourteen miles west of Wapella;[41] and the Scottish crofter colony of experienced farmers at Saltcoats, fifty miles northwest of the Wapella colony.[42] All of these failed by the end of the nineteenth century. In a local

38. *The Jewish Chronicle*, January 19, 1906, p. 16.
39. For a biography of the founder of the Canadian Bronfman family see Hart, p. 169.
40. Brenda J. Stead, *Cannington Manor Historic Park*, Sask. Tourism and Renewable Resources, 3rd ed., 1976, original text by Mrs. A. E. M. Hewlett, 1965.
41. Ruth Humphrys, "Dr. Rudolf Meyer and the French Nobility of Assiniboia," *The Beaver*, Winnipeg, Summer 1978, Outfit 309:1, pp. 16-23.
42. Kent Stuart, "The Scottish Crofter Colony, Saltcoats, 1889-1904," *Saskatchewan History*, vol. XXIV, no. 2, Spring 1971, pp. 41-50. Settled in 1894, by 1899, forty-eight homesteads had been abandoned, and only one of the original homesteaders was on his land.

history of the district, the daughter of a pioneer longtime resident English family, writing about the English settlement north of Wapella neighboring the Russian-Jewish settlement, reported that "by 1900 many of the first English homesteaders left for the towns and cities or returned to their homeland."[43] A 1908 report on Western Canadian Jewish farmers stated that: "The most prosperous Jewish colony in Canada . . . is at Wapella. . . . There are now about fifteen Jewish farmers in this settlement. Starting without any means whatever they are now worth from $10,000 to $40,000 each."[44]

Louis Rosenberg was Manager of Farm Settlements, Western Canada, for the Jewish Colonization Association from 1919 to 1940.[45] In 1928 he reported on thirteen Jewish farmers in the Wapella colony farming 3,520 acres of land:

> While smaller in size, the colony has been quite prosperous of late. Many of the present farmers were born in the colony and were brought up to farming. They are progressive and modern farmers, some of whom have graduated from the agricultural colleges of Manitoba and Saskatchewan. All are engaged in mixed farming and some make a specialty of raising pure bred cattle, horses and sheep.[46]

Rosenberg reported further that this colony has "proved an excellent training ground for young Jewish men desiring to become farmers, and each year several . . . find work in the neighborhood, with a view to becoming established farmers subsequently in other colonies."[47] Fifty years after its founding, reporting on the healthy state of the Jewish farm colonies, he stated: "Wapella remains the oldest existing Jewish farm colony in Western Canada."[48]

The remnant of the Wapella settlement lasted until the

---

43. Kay Surridge, "Woodleigh District," *Mingling Memories: A History of Wapella and Districts* (Wapella, 1979), p. 238.
44. *Montreal Witness*, reprinted in *B'nai B'rith Messenger*, Los Angeles, December 25, 1908, p. 9.
45. In 1891 Baron Maurice de Hirsch, German-Jewish financier and philanthropist, established the Jewish Colonization Association (ICA) to aid in Jewish emigration from Russia and to establish agricultural colonies in North and South America.
46. Rosenberg, "Oldest Farm Colony," p. 22.
47. *Ibid.*
48. Louis Rosenberg, *Canada's Jews: A Social and Economic Study of the Jews in Canada* (Montreal, 1939), p. 219.

1960s when Klenman's younger son had died and Barish' four sons retired, although one fourth generation family descended from the pioneer settlers (Isman-Kaplun) farms in the district to this day.

THE JEWISH FARMERS OF WESTERN CANADA

By Cyril Edel Leonoff

Part II: Attempts at Mass Settlement

Baron Maurice de Hirsch (1831-1896), a German-Jewish financier and industrialist, was the first to plan large-scale resettlement of Jews on the land. His business interests, particularly the skillful engineering of the Oriental Railway scheme linking Constantinople to Europe, and pioneer enterprises in the sugar and copper industries, brought Hirsch's fortune to an estimated $100 million by 1890.[49]

During his work in the Near East Hirsch became aware of the plight of his coreligionists and began to help them. Firmly convinced of the future of the Jews as an agricultural people, Baron de Hirsch wrote:

> My own experience . . . has led me to recognize that the Jews have very good ability in agriculture . . . and my efforts shall show that the Jews have not lost the agricultural qualities that their forefathers possessed. I shall try to make for them a new home in different lands, where as free farmers on their own soil, they can make themselves useful to that country.[50]

In 1891 he established the Baron de Hirsch Fund, in New York, for settling immigrants to the United States (and later Canada), and on September 10, 1891 the Jewish Colonization Association (ICA). The ICA was subscribed to by Jewish leaders in England and Western Europe. It was incorporated as an English stock company, but had its administrative office in Paris. The initial ICA capital of $10 million was increased to $40 million by legacy after the death of Baroness Clara de Hirsch in 1899.[51] The objective was ". . . establishing colonies in various parts of North and South America and other purposes."[52]

Hermann Landau's contribution to Canadian land settlement did not stop at his Wapella experiment. In 1887, when the Hirsches

---

49. *Encyclopedia Judaica*, Vol. 8, p. 505.
50. *Ibid.*, p. 507, quoting from *The Forum*, August 1891.
51. Simon Belkin, *Through Narrow Gates* (Montreal, 1966), pp. 68-69.
52. *Encyclopedia Judaica*, Vol. 8, p. 506.

lost their only son, Landau went to Paris to pay the Baron and Baroness a visit of condolence, and took this occasion to tell the grieving couple "that they could adopt all Israel as their children by founding colonies in Canada, and so rescue a great number of Jews from the persecution they were undergoing at the hands of the autocratic government of Russia."[53]

Shortly after, Landau received a letter from the Baron, in which he approved of this proposal and asked Landau to find "a devoted self-sacrificing committee to carry the scheme into effect." Landau said he could find such a committee among his Anglo-Jewish associates.[54] However, before the creation of the ICA, the funds for such purposes were inadequate. Land settlement experiences in the 1880s both in Canada and the United States were not very encouraging. And there was a fear among Jewish leaders in England, France and America that "too many Jews" might prejudice the position and stability of those already living in these countries. They wanted to help the immigrants, but quietly and on a small scale. Pressed by ensuing events, they subsequently cooperated with Baron de Hirsch.[55]

Contrary to Landau's advice, however, Baron de Hirsch did not turn to Canada as the preferred country for Jewish colonization but concentrated his efforts on Argentina. Apparently the decisive factor was that some 800 Jewish colonists had already settled (in 1889) independently in the Argentine. He was also impressed with the mild climate and good quality of the soil there.[56] Whereas the Baron was unfamiliar with farming conditions in the severe climate of the Canadian Northwest.

In 1891 the Canadian Jewish population was very small, numbering only 6,501.[57] The main Jewish community, comprising about a third of the population, was centered in Montreal. This city was also the main port of entry for European immigrants. During the summer of 1891 alone, as many as 1,500 Jewish ref-

53. "Mr. Hermann Landau on Canada and the Jews," *The Jewish Chronicle*, London, January 19, 1906, p. 16.
54. *Ibid.*
55. Belkin, pp. 65-66.
56. *Ibid.*, p. 68.
57. Louis Rosenberg, *Canada's Jews: A Social and Economic Study of the Jews of Canada* (Montreal, 1939), p. 11.

ugees arrived in a destitute condition.[58] The Young Men's Hebrew Benevolent Society of Montreal at that time was the major philanthropic institution for care of the local Jewish poor, but in 1890-1891 extended its work to include immigrant aid. The established Jewish community faced the "spectre of mass ghettoization" of their fellow Jews. The colonization policy being heavily promoted by the Canadian government for dispersal of refugees throughout the Northwest provided a welcome solution to the large influx of immigrants.[59]

Harris Vineberg, president of the society, a man of broad vision, was informed of conditions out west through relatives there. He advocated the settlement of 1,000 to 2,000 Jewish families (5,000 to 10,000 persons) in Manitoba or the North-West Territories. He further conceived the idea of a mixed economy combining farming and industry in such a colony. To implement this plan, the YMHBS formed a Colonization Committee under the chairmanship of David A. Ansell.[60]

However, the small Jewish community lacked the resources to finance a large-scale venture. Shortly after the YMHBS became aware of the Baron de Hirsch Fund, Vineberg appealed to Hirsch for financial aid. The Baron responded with a contribution of $20,000 part of which was used to purchase a building in Montreal, named the Baron de Hirsch Institute. Housing a school and immigrant shelter, it functioned as the center of the YMHBS's philanthropic activities. Later the society also took this name.[61]

At a meeting of the society held on March 29, 1891 a letter signed by the heads of fifty-one Jewish families residing in Montreal was read. They asked for assistance to go to the Northwest where they would settle on farms.[62] Unable to handle such a request with its own means, several ensuing meetings of the YMHBS board were taken up with discussion of the problem. Finally a resolution

---

58. ICA, London, 371, H. Vineberg, Montreal, to Baron de Hirsch, Paris, October 7, 1891.
59. On the beginnings of YMHBS immigrant aid work and the early years of the Hirsch Colony see Lawrence F. Tapper, "The Jewish Agricultural Colonies of Hirsch and Oxbow, Saskatchewan 1890-1900: A Study in Jewish Frontier Growth," Dissertation, Department of Religion, Carleton University, Ottawa, August 1975, 116 pp.
60. Belkin, p. 59.
61. Ibid., pp. 38-39.
62. Ibid., p. 60.

was passed, "That this society is unable to afford any relief to future arrivals of destitute emigrant Jews . . . until a proper plan of colonization be formulated and the necessary means provided therefor."[63] The Baron responded immediately by forwarding $2,000 for care of the refugees through the Paris-based *Alliance Israelite Universelle.*

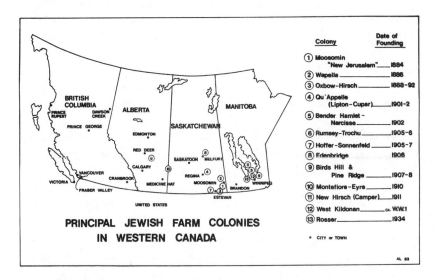

Colony	Date of Founding
(1) Moosomin "New Jerusalem"	1884
(2) Wapella	1886
(3) Oxbow-Hirsch	1888-92
(4) Qu'Appelle (Lipton-Cupar)	1901-2
(5) Bender Hamlet - Narcisse	1902
(6) Rumsey-Trochu	1905-6
(7) Hoffer-Sonnenfeld	1905-7
(8) Edenbridge	1908
(9) Birds Hill & Pine Ridge	1907-8
(10) Montefiore-Eyre	1910
(11) New Hirsch (Camper)	1911
(12) West Kildonan	ca. W.W.1
(13) Rosser	1934

• CITY or TOWN

PRINCIPAL JEWISH FARM COLONIES IN WESTERN CANADA

Then came the news that the ICA was incorporated, giving hope that Canada might be included in its land settlement work. A letter was addressed to Baron de Hirsch giving the opinion of the board that the only permanent solution (with the Baron's co-operation) was to establish a large-scale pattern of colonization "to prove . . . [of] lasting importance to those who are willing to work with industry and diligence in their adopted country."[64]

The YMHBS also sought financial support from the Russo-Jewish Committee through Herman Adler, Chief Rabbi of England. He responded negatively:

> As you know, we have founded, nine years ago, a colony near Moosomin. We contributed 3,000 pounds for settlement

---

63. ICA, 371, Resolution passed at an Extraordinary Meeting of the Board, September 13, 1891.
64. *Ibid.,* Vineberg to Hirsch, October 7, 1891.

and maintenance, and in spite of the fact that we had the benefit of Sir Alexander Galt's information and advice on every step . . . the colony was unfortunately a failure. We therefore did not find ourselves justified to use additional funds for that purpose.[65]

Obviously the London Committee did not have the will for further colonization ventures. In another letter received from the secretary of the Russo-Jewish Committee the YMHBS were advised that the trustees of the Mansion House Fund would be prepared to transfer their interests in the land at Moosomin for the benefit of suitable Russo-Jewish settlers who would be able "to make their way without our assistance."[66]

The ICA expressed an interest in the YMHBS project.[67] Dr. Sigismund Sonnenfeld, director of the ICA, asked for more information on the project's feasibility, particularly the cost to establish a family in the Northwest with cattle, seed, shelter, and food to sustain them during the first year. The Colonization Committee, charged with the planning and implementation of the project, made a thorough investigation and produced its first report,[68] which was accepted by the board on December 13, 1891 with a copy forwarded to the ICA.[69]

In deciding on the cost per family to settle in the Northwest the Colonization Committee relied on the opinions of L. O. Armstrong, Canadian Pacific Railway (CPR) Land Commissioner at Winnipeg and the German Consul there who had supervised the settlement of Mennonites. The consul felt that the cost would be from $690 to $880. However, the committee accepted the minimum estimate of $500 given by Armstrong.[70] This figure proved to be unrealistic for the Jewish colonists who arrived with no money and were totally dependent on the ICA for several years. The committee also recommended the engagement of experienced gentile farmers of English or Scottish origin "in order to give full instructions,

---

65. Public Archives of Canada (PAC), RG 15, 269180 (2), Rev. Dr. H. Adler, London to D. A. Ansell, Montreal, November 10, 1891.
66. Belkin, p. 61.
67. ICA, 371, Vineberg to S. Sonnenfeld, Paris, November 24, 1891.
68. *Ibid.*, "Baron de Hirsch Institute Report of the Colonization Committee," October 1, 1891.
69. *Ibid.*, Vineberg to Sonnenfeld, December 14, 1891.
70. *Ibid.*, L. O. Armstrong, CPR, Winnipeg to Vineberg, Dec. 10, 1891.

and to assist in cultivating the land properly."[71] In a letter dated January 27, 1892 Dr. Sonnenfeld advised that the sum of $30,000, sufficient to install sixty families, could be procured in Paris.[72]

In January 1892 the Colonization Committee waited on J. J. C. Abbott, the Canadian Prime Minister who had replaced Macdonald after his death, and John Carling, Minister of Agriculture, to solicit the government's cooperation in establishing the

A pioneer barn of adobe, built by Yankle Pollack, on the modern farm of Harvey and Jack Kleiman, Hirsch, Saskatchewan.

proposed Jewish colony. Abbott "decidedly viewed with favour the undertaking . . . and would assist them as far as possible."[73] Later Abbott confirmed that "it is most important to secure such a large influx of immigrants."[74]

At a separate meeting W. H. Baker, clerk to the YMHBS board, met with Edgar Dewdney, Minister of the Interior, who was the minister responsible for colonization, his deputy A. M.

---

71. *Ibid.*, "Report of the Colonization Committee to the Board of Directors of the YMHBS," December 13, 1891.
72. Belkin, p. 70.
73. ICA, 371, "The Colonization Committee's Report of the Deputation, of D. Ansell, S. Davis, M. Goldstein and W. H. Baker to the Prime Minister, J. J. C. Abbott and Hon. John Carling, Minister of Agriculture, Monday, January 11, 1892."

Burgess, and John Lowe, Deputy Minister of Agriculture. Burgess was strongly against bloc colonization, favoring colonization on alternate sections, which "created a feeling of emulation when different nationalities were mixed together."[75] Citing the failure of the Icelanders in Manitoba to combine farming with fishing, he disapproved of the board's desire to combine farming and industry,[76] which they felt would provide the colonists with winter employment. Burgess, who was considered the authority on colonization, was probably wrong. Establishment of rural clothing factories helped to stabilize the economy of the contemporary farm colonies in New Jersey,[77] and introduction of industry in later times has proved of economic benefit to many kibbutzim in Israel.

With the financial support of Baron de Hirsch practically assured, and the favorable reaction of the senior Canadian Government officials, early in 1892 the YMHBS was ready to launch its colonization project. David Ansell was sent to Europe to promote the scheme.[78] Then came the question of land. Unrealistically dreaming of their "grandiose plan," they wanted to know if the government had homestead land available for 2,000 families or 10,000 people.[79] Burgess, who considered the land in the Northwest to be the best in the world, recommended the more remote Prince Albert, Red Deer, and Edmonton districts.[80] He cautioned the committee "that the selection of lands for settlement should be made by the intending settlers themselves or through their agents."[81] Consideration was also given to the Russo-Jewish Committee land near Moosomin, and to land immediately south of Regina recommended by the government immigration agent there.

The board sent two non-Jews, Charles McDiarmid, a practical farmer, the newly-appointed manager of the colony, and Ignatius Roth, superintendent of the Baron de Hirsch Institute, to scout the

---

74. PAC, RG 15, 269180 (2), J. J. C. Abbott, Ottawa to J. Lowe, Ottawa, January 11, 1892.
75. ICA, 371, "Supplementary Report of the Deputation." Baker's meeting with E. Dewdney, A. M. Burgess and J. Lowe, Jan. 11, 1892.
76. Ibid.
77. Joseph Brandes, Immigrants to Freedom: Jewish Communities in Rural New Jersey Since 1882 (Philadelphia, 1971), pp. 144-169.
78. ICA, 371, Vineberg to Sonnenfeld, January 18, 1892.
79. PAC RG 15, 269180 (2), Baker, Montreal to Abbott, January 16, 1892.
80. Ibid., Burgess, Ottawa to Abbott, January 26, 1892.
81. Ibid., J. Carling, Ottawa to Baker, January 20, 1892.

proposed locations. The delegates liked the lands near Moosomin and Regina. But they reported that the buildings of the first settlers on the Moosomin farms had been destroyed, the cultivated land had reverted to prairie, and the district was still twenty-five miles away from the nearest railroad. The Regina land was bare and lacked wooded areas for use as firewood.[82]

Tiferes Israel School, one of three public schools
that served the Qu'Appelle Colony, Saskatchewan.

In 1888 the CPR had started to build a branch line from Brandon, Manitoba to the coal mines near Estevan in the Assiniboia district (now in the southeast corner of Saskatchewan). This brought a number of Jewish storekeepers and farmers to the towns arising along the railroad. One, Jacob Pierce, and his sons settled near Oxbow where they farmed and operated a store in the village. They were joined by a number of other Jewish families and a small

82. Belkin, p. 71.

Jewish farm community sprang up.[83] Acting on the advice of Asher Pierce, the Colonization Committee was persuaded by the benefits of the established Jewish farmers nearby, the presence of the railway and availability of cheap fuel.

McDiarmid selected Township 3, Range 5, west of the second land surveyors' meridian, nineteen miles east of Estevan and twenty-one miles west of Oxbow, and some lands in adjacent townships. The committee wanted to have the Jewish settlers as close together as possible to provide for their social and religious needs. The reservation of the even-numbered sections in that township and some communal pasture was the main concession granted by the Dominion Government. The colony and the railway station were named Hirsch in honor of Baron de Hirsch.[84]

After Ansell's visit, Dr. Sonnenfeld cabled early in March that "the Alliance and Baron de Hirsch would place the sum of 100,000 francs [$20,000] at the disposal of the YMHBS for the installation of colonists."[85] It was noted that it was impossible to provide further aid. The board, who had already selected eighty-four families, was extremely disappointed by the reduced funds, which were sufficient only for forty families.[86] Nevertheless they decided to proceed with the project.[87] The prospective colonists were carefully screened as to their suitability for pioneering life. They were to be "competent, able or willing to work on the land and become practical and useful farmers."[88]

Nineteen teams of horses were purchased in Montreal and shipped to the colony site. Arrangements were made to purchase a like number of oxen. A supply of wagons and farm implements was purchased at Brandon. On April 27, 1892, twenty-seven heads of families left Montreal by rail for Oxbow, arriving on May 2. From Oxbow they made the twenty-mile trek over poor roads to the colony site. The first group was followed by a second from Montreal as well as a few settlers from Winnipeg and Regina, making forty-nine families in all. The women and children remained in

83. *Ibid.*, p. 58.
84. *Ibid.*, pp. 71-72.
85. *Ibid.*, p. 71
86. ICA, 371, Report of S. Davis, Acting Chairman of the Colonization Committee to Sonnenfeld, March 8, 1892.
87. *Ibid.*, Vineberg to Sonnenfeld, April 5, 1892.
88. *Ibid.*, Vineberg to Sonnenfeld, February 11, 1892.

Montreal under the care of the Colonization Committee until the men could build some houses on the homesteads. They arrived at the colony in October.[89] Public opinion in Canada was impressed with the undertaking. Favorable comment was expressed in the press. One newspaper closed its remarks with a prayer, "God help the poor Jews."[90]

By July, when homesteads were taken up for sons, other relatives and friends, the YMHBS had a total of seventy-three home-

European style gravehouses at the Jewish
farm colony near Lipton, Saskatchewan.

steads covering 12,160 acres under its direction. That summer, when an additional twelve families came out on their own and took up adjoining lands, the colony swelled to eighty-five homesteads occupying 13,600 acres.[91] The Hirsch funds could not be stretched to provide enough for everyone. Implements and livestock had to be shared. The colonists fought among themselves and with their managers for the scarce resources. In the fall the Baron acceded to the board's request and furnished an additional $16,500.[92] Further sums were disbursed later.

In its first three years the colony was a dismal failure. The

89. Belkin, p. 72.
90. *Ibid.*, quoting *Canadian Gleaner*, May 26, 1892.
91. Tapper, Chapter II, pp. 4-5.
92. ICA, 371, L. A. Hart, President YMHBS, Montreal to Sonnenfeld, November 2, 1892.

colonists' farming ignorance was as great as the society's management ineptitude. The colony was administered by a well-meaning
but inexperienced committee in Montreal, 1,700 miles away. From
the beginning they had vastly underestimated the difficulties and
capital needed for placing novice farmers on the land. And progress was hindered by a series of inept field managers.[93]

The colony was dependent on the financial support of a
philanthropic organization in Paris, who knew little about the costs
of establishing and servicing a pioneer community in Canada.
From April 1892 through 1894 the ICA had pumped a total of
$65,000 into the colony with little to show for it.[94] Baron de Hirsch
did not consider this venture to be one of pure philanthropy. In
order for the colonists to become self-sufficient he felt that they
had to learn responsibility. So he required them to pay back their
loans by way of a mortgage on their properties.[95] This raised the
ire of the farmers, many of whom were unable or unwilling to
pay.[96]

Worst of all, the region was beset by unfortunate climatic
conditions, resulting in three years of successive crop failures.
Drought, hail and grasshopper plagues followed one another. Many
of the colonists abandoned their homesteads. Some of them drifted
to the more populous Oxbow district. This move was also caused
by the lack of schools in the colony. But a core of hardened colonists could not be dislodged no matter how great the hardship.[97]
Their saga is a story of heroic proportions in the annals of pioneer
settlement of the Canadian West.

In the fall of 1895 the colony's fortunes began to turn with
the harvest of its first bumper crop.[98] The prosperity continued
through 1896 with another bountiful harvest and increase of livestock to thirty-five horses and 127 head of cattle. A number of
settlers had returned to their homesteads. There had been two marriages and three births. And the population was augmented by the
arrival of five new families from Red Deer.[99] The community now

93. Tapper, Chapter II, pp. 3-30.
94. *Ibid.*, Chapter II, p. 27.
95. PAC, RG 15, 644, 269180 (1), O'Reilley Jarvis, Homestead Inspector, Oxbow,
    to H. H. Smith, Commissioner of Dominion Lands, Winnipeg, June 28, 1893.
96. Tapper, Chapter II, pp. 10-16.
97. *Ibid.*, Chapter II, p. 25, Chapter III, pp. 3-4.
98. *Ibid.*, Chapter II, p. 25.
99. *Ibid.*, p. 28.

consisted of twenty-three families and the colony was finally on its way to stabilization.

Baron de Hirsch had died in April 1896 and control of the ICA passed to a Council of Administration. In September 1896 Ansell was so optimistic about the results of that season that he asked the council to send out additional colonists to occupy the vacant homesteads.[100] The council was cautious, and before making a decision to proceed, sought impartial advice from its affiliate, the Baron de Hirsch Fund of New York.[101] In June 1897 Professor

Instructor Harry Barish (right) of Wapella examining quality of seed grain being sown at Sonnenfeld Colony, Saskatchewan, c. 1926.

H. L. Sabsovich, Superintendent of the Woodbine Colony, New Jersey, was sent out to report on farming conditions in the district, the reasons for failure of the colony, and the best means for re-establishing it.

Sabsovich was favorably impressed with the Hirsch district. He recommended the immediate purchase of a threshing machine to take off the crop, livestock raising with a creamery, and the establishment of schools with a Hebrew teacher. The schools could also be used for worship on Saturdays and Holy Days. He further

100. ICA, 372, Ansell to ICA, Paris, September 7, 1896.
101. ICA, 490, Sonnenfeld to Central Committee, Baron de Hirsch Fund, New York, November 19, 1896.

recommended that administration of the colony be taken over from the YMHBS by the Baron de Hirsch Fund, with a resident manager in Canada.[102] At the ICA meeting of October 24, 1897, the council accepted the substance of Sabsovich's report and decided to place $15,000 at the disposal of the YMHBS for settlement of forty families. Funds were also allocated for the threshing machine, the creamery, two schools and the teachers' salaries.[103] After protracted negotiations, it took the ICA another two years to effect transfer of the colony from the YMHBS.[104]

In June 1899 Sim Alfred Goldston arrived from London, England to take charge of the Hirsch schools.[105] Born in London in 1873, the son of a rabbi, he received a thorough Jewish education as well as a general education at King's College.[106] Later he was editor of the early Anglo-Jewish newspapers in British Columbia.[107] On August 1, 1899 the first Jewish school in Western Canada, giving both secular and religious instruction, opened in the village of Hirsch with an enrollment of thirty pupils.[108] It also served as the synagogue. Later a second school and synagogue was opened in the northern part of the colony. The schools were named Ansell and Vineberg in honor of the colony's prime movers. When the Province of Saskatchewan was formed in 1905, and assumed control of public education, the schools were turned over to the local public school districts. In April 1905 a young man twenty-two years of age, James Garfield Gardiner, arrived at Hirsch on his first teaching appointment. Teaching his school of forty-four pupils, "two Canadians, two Norwegians, the remaining forty Jewish, of Russian or Rumanian origin"[109] must surely have been a unique experience. He also served as English translator and secretary for the largely Yiddish-speaking colony.[110] "Jimmy" Gardiner was later to gain eminence as Premier of Saskatchewan,

102. ICA, 484, Report of H. L. Sabsovich, 1897.
103. ICA, London, Seance du Conseil d'Administration du 24 October 1897, p. 39.
104. Tapper, Chapter III, pp. 10-25.
105. *Ibid.*, p. 14.
106. Arthur D. Hart, ed., *The Jew in Canada* (Toronto and Montreal, 1926), p. 178.
107. Cyril Edel Leonoff, *Pioneers, Pedlars, and Prayer Shawls: The Jewish Communities in British Columbia and the Yukon* (Victoria, 1978), p. 146.
108. ICA, 372, Report of Baker's visit to Hirsch, July-August 1899.
109. Nathaniel A. Benson, *None of it Came Easy: The Story of James Garfield Gardiner* (Toronto, 1955), p. 82.
110. *Ibid.*, pp. 66-69.

and federal Minister of Agriculture for twenty-two years. Throughout his career he maintained a lifelong friendship with the Jewish people.[111]

Saskatchewan Pool elevators built in 1928 at the village
of Oungre, named for Dr. Louis Oungre, general manager
of the Jewish Colonization Association.

Other steps were taken to revitalize the colony. In the spring of 1899 the ICA decided to send a vanguard of ten Boryslaw miners from Galicia to work in the coal mines.[112] Illustrative of the resurgence of the colony, a problem developed when, after viewing the now prosperous farms, they asked to take up farming instead of mining.[113] In July money was allocated for the settlement of twelve youths as farm apprentices.[114] A far-reaching move was made in November 1899 when a group of fifteen Russian

111. *Ibid.*, pp. 70-71.
112. ICA, Seance du Conseil d'Administration du 12 Mars 1899, p. 85.
113. Tapper, Chapter III, p. 18.
114. *Ibid.*

33

Jewish families under the leadership of Rabbi Marcus Berner, who had settled earlier that year near Yorkton,[115] were relocated to the colony. Rabbi-farmer Marcus Berner, trained in England, served the Hirsch community for thirty-two years as rabbi, *schochet*, chairman of the school board and municipal councillor. For the last ten years of his life Rabbi Berner was spiritual leader at historic Congregation Emanu-El in Victoria, British Columbia.[116] He is acknowledged as the preeminent pioneer rabbi of Western Canada.[117]

By 1900 the colony was well on the road to recovery. In that year the ICA took direct control, and in 1903 transferred authority to its American agents, the Jewish Agricultural Society of New York. Hirsch colony never achieved the large scale of development envisioned by its planners. Yet it persisted as a stable Jewish farm community for half a century. On the fiftieth anniversary of Jewish settlement in Western Canada, Louis Rosenberg reported on Hirsch:

> Although the number of Jewish men, women and children in the colony remains almost the same as it was thirty-eight years ago, the acreage under cultivation has increased to almost 10,000 . . . horses to 250, cattle to 200, and the value of implements to over $33,000. The annual crop yield . . . has reached 70,000 bushels of wheat, 30,000 bushels of oats, 40,000 bushels of barley, and 10,000 bushels of flax.[118]

Some Jewish farmers have continued to farm in the Oxbow-Hirsch district to this day. The principal Jewish farmers remaining at Hirsch are brothers Harvey and Jack Kleiman, who farm eighteen quarter-sections (2,880 acres) of land.

In 1897, when Canada's new Liberal Prime Minister Sir Wilfrid Laurier came to London to participate in Queen Victoria's Diamond Jubilee, he was questioned by Hermann Landau about his attitude to Jewish settlement. Laurier stated that, if the Jews were serious about their land settlement plans, Canada would welcome their immigration and would afford facilities for their set-

115. ICA, Seance du Conseil d'Administration du 20 Mais 1899, p. 90.
116. Rosenberg, "Rabbi Marcus Berner," *The Jewish Western Bulletin*, Vancouver, June 30, 1958, p. 12, reprinted from *The Israelite Press*, Winnipeg, June 1941.
117. Abraham Arnold, "The First Rabbis in Saskatchewan," *The Western Jewish News*, Winnipeg, October 2, 1980, p. 3.
118. Rosenberg, "Jews in Agriculture in Western Canada," *The Israelite Daily Press*, 50th Anniversary of the Jew in the West ed., 1882-1932, p. 55.

tlement on the land. He further promised that "the Dominion will grant the Jews such a measure of self-government as will enable them to make their own by-laws substituting Saturday for Sunday."[119]

At the beginning of the twentieth century a second mass exodus of European Jews began, this time from Roumania. This emigration resulted from political intimidation, barring Jews from the public schools and the professions, from work in state institutions, and from the selling of commodities. In 1899, almost spontaneously, many thousands called "the walkers" set out on foot as far as Hamburg with the goal of reaching North America. Up to World War I, 70,000 Jews left Roumania.[120] Like the Russian Jews, no job was too hard for them. Many accepted jobs as unskilled workers.

Undeterred by the difficulties at the Hirsch Colony the ICA, acting on Laurier's pronouncement, decided to proceed with another colonization attempt in Canada. Large numbers of these Roumanians had come to London enroute. Barred from the United States, which had a policy forbidding entry to such assisted immigrants, many were turning to Canada. In the summer of 1900 Alfred L. Cohen, a prominent London Jew, on behalf of the ICA corresponded on this subject with Lord Revelstoke, the Colonial Secretary. Cohen had been in touch with W. Preston, Canadian immigration agent in London who advised that the Dominion Government was prepared to welcome able-bodied immigrants suitable for homesteading in the Northwest, and had expressed the opinion that the Dominion would make a grant of townships to the ICA for this purpose.

Cohen pointed out that the ICA was willing to help "suitable emigrants." They desired to avoid increasing "the alien immigration into England and add to the congestion in the east of London, and they are even more anxious to avoid sending to Canada unsuitable emigrants who will infiltrate into the Canadian towns." Cohen stated that the ICA was only interested in assisting such a project if it was properly organized so that the settlers would not become a continuous charge on the association. It was "absolutely

---

119. Landau, "Canada and the Jews," p. 16.
120. *Encyclopedia Judaica*, Vol. 14, p. 390.

indispensable" to establish these settlers under capable management since most of them "have been engaged in urban pursuits and have little experience of agriculture." He also urged "that a rigid . . . selection as to their physique, morality and condition" be made.[121] Revelstoke referred the letter to Lord Minto, the Canadian Governor-General, with the request that the matter be dealt with as favorably as possible by the Canadian Government.[122]

On July 21st Preston and Israel Tarte, the Canadian Government representative in Paris, attended a conference in that city of delegates from various European countries convened to discuss the Roumanian refugee crisis. They were asked if Canada would agree to accept in the following year "a number of agriculturists from among the Roumanian Jews." Preston made it clear that Canada desired to admit "only intending agriculturists." Tarte promised to present their request to the Canadian Minister of the Interior. He was given a guarantee that the ICA would provide funds to the extent of eighty to 100 pounds per immigrant for expenses for farm settlement.[123]

In November Cohen wrote to Minto advising that he had received a letter from James A. Smart, Canadian Deputy Minister of the Interior, who wrote "somewhat less sympathetically than your Lordship." Cohen advised that Preston intended to go to Roumania to see the situation for himself. Cohen felt that Preston's report would "modify Mr. Smart's opinion." He also stated that arrangements were being made to teach the immigrants some English. Cohen recommended "a suitable resident inspector, not a theorist but a practical man who would take charge of their installation."[124]

The proposals of Alfred Cohen and the Paris meeting were forwarded to the Department of the Interior in Ottawa on December 10, 1900. Smart submitted his views on the subject in a confidential memorandum to Minister Clifford Sifton. Smart ad-

121. PAC, RG 7, G 18, vol. 100 (4) Governor General's External Affairs, A. L. Cohen, London to Lord Revelstoke, London, July 13, 1900.
122. Ibid., Revelstoke to Lord Minto, London, July 13, 1900.
123. PAC, MG 27 II, D 16, vol. 15, Tarte Papers: Colonization 1900-05, W. Preston, London to Lord Strathcona, Canadian High Commissioner, London, July 27, 1900, with copy and covering note to I. Tarte, Paris, July 28, 1900.
124. PAC, Governor General's External Affairs, Cohen to Minto, Ottawa, November 10, 1900.

vised that without some previous agricultural experience these people "would not likely succeed in the Canadian northwest." Preston had reported on his findings in Roumania that only a very small proportion of the people "know anything at all of farm life," but with "proper selection and medical examination . . . it might be well to try the experiment." Smart dismissed Preston's plan as "entirely unworkable." Smart wrote that "there is nothing . . . to prevent a few from coming if they have enough means to enable them to settle on farms." However, he opposed bringing "this class of people" to Canada "in large number."[125]

Four months later Sifton forwarded a copy of Smart's memorandum to Prime Minister Laurier. In a confidential covering note of his own Sifton stated, "experience shows that the Jewish people do not become agriculturists. However strong the attempts . . . to induce them to remain upon the land . . . such efforts have . . . proved an undoubted failure."[126] At the same time, true to his previous words, the Prime Minister conveyed the government's view to Lord Minto:

> I have not forgotten the answer to be sent to Lord Revelstoke about Jewish immigration. I have asked the Department . . . to recast the paper which they had prepared. I want them to make it clear, that whilst the doors of this country are open to all we favor only agricultural immigration.[127]

The agreement finally worked out between the ICA and the Canadian Government included these terms: the Canadian immigration agent in London would select a number of Roumanian Jewish families; the ICA would pay for their transportation; all settlement arrangements would be made by the Canadian Minister of the Interior; the ICA agreed to deposit with the Canadian Government 1,000 francs ($200) per family for the purchase of livestock, farming equipment, building material, etc. to be disbursed by the Deputy Minister at his discretion; management of the colony would be undertaken by the Department; within two years from the date of settlement, when the immigrants were expected to be

---

125. *Ibid.*, J. Smart, Ottawa, to C. Sifton, Ottawa, December 10, 1900.
126. *Ibid.*, Sifton to W. Laurier, Ottawa, April 15, 1901.
127. PAC, MG 27 II Bi, vol. 5, Minto Papers, Laurier to Minto, April 13, 1901.

self-supporting, they would commence repayment of loans advanced to them.[128]

The plan proved to be far from satisfactory in practice. The Deputy Minister had no intention of giving his personal attention to the project. He delegated responsibility to D. H. McDonald of Fort Qu'Appelle, a prominent figure of the day in the North-West Territories, who owned the local bank and many of the stores. A site for settlement was chosen twenty-five miles north of the nearest railway station at Qu'Appelle and seventy miles northeast of Regina. The colony, occupying an area of 8,408 acres, was spread out, twenty-five miles from south to north and eighteen miles from east to west. This made communication among the settlers difficult. The slightly-rolling land, broken up by numerous sloughs fringed with clumps of willow and poplar trees, was admirably suited to mixed farming. But the land was too much cut up by the sloughs, and the annual frost-free period averaged only ninety days, too short for the best wheat growing.

The first group of forty-nine families, comprising 100 persons, arrived at Qu'Appelle in the spring of 1901. Shortly after their arrival the little encampment was stricken by an epidemic of diphtheria. Some weeks passed before the settlers were sufficiently recovered to proceed to the allotted lands. There, under the guidance of half-breed Indians from nearby reservations, they learned to erect log houses chinked with clay and roofed with sod. They ploughed up a few acres each for potatoes and put up some hay for the winter.

The supervisors appointed by McDonald were local non-Jewish farmers and businessmen who, "even had they been free from anti-Jewish prejudice, were incapable of making themselves understood by the Jewish settlers, as they had no knowledge of either Yiddish or Roumanian, or even German. The neighbors and the supervisors despised the newcomers, and looked upon the entire scheme as a costly joke, doomed to failure." Much of the money, which had been intended for the purchase of farm equipment, was squandered by the supervisors in doles of flour, sugar, beans and meat. As a result the settlers were without sufficient horses, oxen, and machinery to work the land and so become self-

---

128. "Report of Jewish Colonization Association — Central Administration, for 1902-1903."

sufficient. When the funds ran out, and the supervisors cut down the food doles, chaos resulted.[129]

Many of the immigrants were unsuited for pioneering and soon left the colony. But their numbers were replenished by a second group which arrived from Roumania in August 1901, and by a third group which came in 1902. The total number of persons brought over under this scheme was 365.[130] Many of the colonists were demoralized. Some looked upon the equipment and livestock supplied to them as gifts and did not feel obligated to undertake repayment.

By April 1903, when the Deputy Minister had asked to be relieved of responsibility, the ICA requested the Jewish Agricultural Society of New York to investigate conditions in the colony and to assume its administration. The first survey of the colony made by the society in 1903-1904 showed the lack of progress: only 500 acres were under cultivation; there were only forty-nine horses, fifty-three milk cows, and fifty-one head of other cattle.[131] Under the new administration the colony was reorganized on a productive basis. Undesirable elements among the population were weeded out. Additional loans were advanced to the farmers for the purchase of livestock and implements. The colony attracted some Jewish immigrants from Russia who contributed some farming experience and considerable capital of their own.

In 1906 a branch line of the CPR was extended northwestward and the village of Lipton sprang up at the nearest station, fourteen miles from the heart of the colony. That portion of the settlement nearest the village took the name Lipton, while the northwesterly portion took the name Cupar, which was the nearest railway station to it. Thus the old name Qu'Appelle Colony fell into disuse. Three public schools named Herzl, Tiferes Israel and Yeshurun were erected, a Hebrew teacher and a *schochet* were engaged. A cemetery was consecrated, and a synagogue building was erected in the village of Lipton.

Under these conditions the fortunes of the colony began to change. Statistics in the early 1930s showed: almost 14,000 acres

---

129. Rosenberg, "Jews in Agriculture," pp. 55-56. Rosenberg was a school teacher in the colony and collected its early history.
130. Belkin, p. 77.
131. *Ibid.*

under cultivation; machinery valued at \$25,000; 200 horses; and 230 head of cattle. Crop yield averaged 35,000 bushels of wheat, 10,000 bushels of oats, 2,000 bushels of barley and 10,000 bushels of rye.[132] In recent years only the occasional Jewish farmer is to be found in the Lipton District. Some of the Lipton families have been engaged in cattle feed lots and an abattoir on the outskirts of Regina. A Lipton son, Sol Sinclair, has gained prominence as professor of agricultural economics and farm management at the University of Manitoba.

In the first decade of the 1900s increasing unrest in the Russian Empire, the Russo-Japanese War of 1904-1905, and the bloody pogroms of April 1903 and October 1905 in Kishinev,[133] caused an accelerating emigration of Jews. The aftermath of the 1905 pogrom was another occasion where Sir Wilfrid Laurier expressed friendly sentiments towards the Jewish people. He rose in the House of Commons to protest against Czarist Russia, saying that Canada was open to the Jews of Russia and other lands and would receive them as honored guests.[134] At a public protest meeting held in Ottawa he made an eloquent appeal for subscriptions to a relief fund for the pogrom victims, and was quoted as saying: "We cannot bring all the Jews of that country to Canada, but we can extend a hearty welcome to those who choose to come to these shores!"[135] The Laurier government was doing everything possible to attract large numbers of immigrants to Canada, and among these, Jews were arriving in increasing numbers. The rise of a substantial Jewish community in the fast-growing Dominion became a reality.

As the government continued to open new districts for settlement and the news of "free land" spread in Eastern Europe, many Jews came to Canada with the avowed purpose of becoming farmers. They came on their own initiative and established themselves by their own means. As a result, a half-dozen independent Jewish colonies sprang up in Western Canada, two each in Manitoba, Saskatchewan and Alberta. About as many Jewish farmers estab-

132. Rosenberg. "Jews in Agriculture," p. 56.
133. *Encyclopedia Judaica*, Vol. 10, pp. 1064-1066.
134. Belkin, p. 78.
135. *Canadian Jewish Year Book*, 1941-42, p. 93, quoted by H. Wolofsky, *The Jewish Chronicle*, December 1, 1905.

lished outside of the colonies, singly or in small groups, over the vast expanse of the Canadian Northwest. As with other ethnic groups of the time several Jews had insufficient capital, or chose the wrong land, and thus did not succeed in farming. Other Jewish families did become deeply rooted in the virgin soil of Western Canada.

Hoffer-Sonnenfeld, founded in 1905-1907 in Southern Saskatchewan, was a fortunate amalgam of private enterprise Jewish farmers, some of whom had trained in farming methods before coming to the site, along with the assistance of the now-experienced and well organized Jewish Colonization Association. In contrast to the earlier established ICA-YMHBS Hirsch Colony and the ICA-Government Qu'Appelle Colony, it became a thriving community of unquestioned success, and remained so past the midpoint of this century.

In 1905 the ICA sent to Canada, at its expense, a group of young men trained at its agricultural school in Slobodka-Lesna, Galicia.[136] They went to established farms at Hirsch and Wapella to obtain Canadian farming experience, to receive instruction in the English language, and to build up some capital in order to start out on their own. Israel Hoffer has described the beginning of the colony:

> I . . . organized a group, including Philip Berger, [Majer] Feldman, Max Feuer and myself,[137] to set up a settlement of our own. The site in tp. 2, rg 15, W 2nd, was decided upon, after some exploration, because the land was pretty well vacant, the closest neighbors being twenty miles east, so that we could establish a Jewish settlement without difficulty.[138]

They also liked the quality of the soil, "a chocolate loam . . . as good as the average in Saskatchewan." The land was in the short grass plains, treeless, but the farmers had to remove tons of stones before they were able to break up their land. The site was forty miles due west of Estevan and sixty miles from Hirsch.

Although Israel Hoffer filed homestead claims in November

---

136. This was a four-year course with half the day spent in classroom studies and half in practical experience on the college's farms.
137. For biographies of these men and their families see Souris Valley No. 7 History Club, *The Saga of Souris Valley*: RM No. 7, Oungre, 1976; Berger pp. 650-651; Feldman pp. 656-658: Feuer pp. 98-99; Hoffer pp. 244-246.
138. "Reminiscences of Mr. Israel Hoffer," *Saskatchewan History*, Vol. V, No. 1, winter 1952, pp. 28-32.

1905 for himself, and in proxy for his father Moses and brother Mayer,[139] because of the lack of money the Hoffers did not occupy the land until the spring of 1907. (Israel Hoffer earned only $125 in his first year at Hirsch.) By that time he had brought out his relatives to Canada. The pioneering beginnings of what was to become one of the best farm operations in Southern Saskatchewan are vividly described by Israel Hoffer:

> I bought a team of broncos and harness in June 1907, mostly on credit, and accompanied by my father and brother, went out to homestead. We took with us . . . a milch cow and calf and from these built our cattle herd. I returned to Hirsch for the harvest . . . but the crop was badly frozen.
>
> Our staple food[s] . . . were flour, corn meal, sugar, syrup, tea, coffee and dried peas. We made butter and cheese and ate duck eggs secured from the numerous sloughs in the vicinity.
>
> As there were no trees . . . I attempted to put up a sod house. I had no experience. . . . In one day I had walls up . . . but next morning I found they had all caved in.
>
> The sod house being a failure, I bought a shack that had been abandoned six miles away . . . [and moved] it to my homestead. . . . It was built of one-ply lumber and was not shingled. One night during a violent thunderstorm, the rain poured into the shack so that to keep dry my father and I had to stand in one corner under a twelve-inch board. . . . I went to Estevan where I bought shingles and tar paper, and with some difficulty we shingled the roof. A pretty good job was made of the barn, the first building we built ourselves. For the roof of the [sod] barn we used two-by-fours as rafters and through these wove willow bushes.
>
> All grain from the settlement had to be hauled to Estevan and most supplies bought there. . . . The round trip . . . ordinarily required two and one-half to three days and involved camping on the trail. . . . During the first summer . . . we depended on buffalo bones and chips for fuel but with the coming of fall, we began to haul coal from Estevan.[140]

By 1909 the Jewish colonists owned 6,400 acres of land, but only 376 acres were broken. In 1910 there were sixty-six people living on twenty-seven farms.[141] The colony had fifty horses, sixteen milk cows, and thirty-three head of other cattle. By 1916,

---

139. *Souris Valley*, pp. 247-248.
140. I. Hoffer, "Reminiscences," p. 29.
141. PAC, Box 374, Microfilm Reel A 938, "Report on New Herman," October 1909.

before the ICA became directly involved in the settlement, there were forty-five independent farms with a population of 147 and total acreage of 11,040.[142]

In January 1910 the first council meeting of Souris Valley Municipality No. 7, in which the colony was located, was held. By 1911 the railhead was only twenty miles away. Each homesteader had over thirty acres of land under cultivation. By then the social institutions, which contributed much to the colony's stability and success, were being organized, family life was developing, and survival of the community was assured. The colony started with essentially no women, and the young men were anxious to find mates. Berger married Feldman's sister and Feldman married Berger's sister. Some of the pioneers found wives in the other Jewish colonies.[143] In 1909 Israel Hoffer married Clara Schwartz, whose family was homesteading in the Lipton Colony.[144] A talented, matriarchal figure, she authored two books on interesting episodes in the lives of the Hoffer and Lipton colonies.[145]

A building housing the synagogue, Hebrew school, and accommodation for the man who was both Hebrew teacher and *schochet* was completed in 1912. The building was also the community center. It was here that charitable functions raised money, ladies held their afternoon teas, young people met for box socials, meetings for the Young People's Cultural Club were convened, and dances were held attended by everyone. Two public schools, one with a high school department, served the colony. In 1917, with a modest capital fund of $2,000 and the aid of the ICA, the Jewish Farmer's Cooperative Credit Union of Sonnenfeld was founded with Moses Hoffer, president.[146] A community council was established to deal with Jewish community affairs and Hoffer Sr. served as president throughout his lifetime.[147] Jewish people also served

142. Compiled by Louis Rosenberg, ICA File, Archives of the Canadian Jewish Congress, Montreal.
143. Anna Feldman, "Sonnenfeld — Elements of Survival and Success of a Jewish Farming Community on the Prairies 1905-1939," *Journal*, Canadian Jewish Historical Society, Vol. 6, No. 1, Spring, 1982, p. 42.
144. I. Hoffer, "Reminiscences," p. 31.
145. Clara Hoffer and F. H. Kahan, *Land of Hope* (Saskatoon, 1960); C. Hoffer, *Township Twenty-Five: West of 2nd Meridian, Range 13, Section 10* (Regina, 1974).
146. Feldman, p. 43.
147. *Ibid.*, p. 41.

the general community as municipal councillors, chairmen and trustees of the school boards, and postmasters.[148] Israel Hoffer was appointed Justice of the Peace in 1912.[149] Mayer and Israel Hoffer served as chairmen of the rural telephone company after it was organized in 1916.[150]

Over twenty years elapsed before the long-awaited branch line of the CPR was completed through the heart of the colony in 1927. Three villages, Oungre, Hoffer and Ratcliffe arose along the railway,[151] containing grain elevators, post offices, stores, kosher butcher shops, livery stables, garages and machine shops, lumber yards, etc. to serve the community. Hoffer was named by the railway in appreciation for assistance given by the Hoffer brothers during building of the line. By this time the Hoffer family owned altogether eighteen quarter-sections (2,880 acres) of land.[152] Oungre was built on ICA lands. On August 6, 1928 the municipal council officially adopted the name in honor of Dr. Louis Oungre, ICA General Manager. In return for the favor, the ICA donated free sites for the school and community hall, and made a $500 contribution to the hall's building fund.[153] The colony officially became known as Sonnenfeld, named for Dr. Sigismund Sonnenfeld, first director of the ICA.

During the 1920s there was a continued movement of Russo-Roumanian immigrants to Canada. An attempt was made to settle some of them as farm colonists in Western Canada. Not being able to find a suitable block of land, the ICA decided to enlarge the principal colonies in Saskatchewan. The plan was to gradually increase each settlement to at least 150 families, thus giving the colonies greater stability. In all, sixty-one quarter-sections were purchased, totaling 9,760 acres in Sonnenfeld, Hirsch and Edenbridge colonies, and along with some abandoned farms, were sufficient to install forty to fifty new farmers. The first purchases of land were made in the Sonnenfeld Colony in 1925, and were continued during the following years. The ICA's confidence in the quality of this land was reinforced by the excellent wheat harvest

148. *Souris Valley*, pp. 1-3, 237-238.
149. I. Hoffer, "Reminiscences," p. 32.
150. *Souris Valley*, p. 3.
151. Feldman, p. 45.
152. I. Hoffer, "Reminiscences," p. 31.
153. *Souris Valley*, p. 366.

44

of 1926 and the favorable assessment of Professor A. H. Joel, Chief of the Soil Department at the University of Saskatchewan, who prepared the first soil maps of the province.[154]

Up to this time the ICA had not been involved in the founding or management, or in any significant land transactions in Sonnenfeld, its assistance being limited to advancing loans to farmers or institutions.[155] The purchase now of forty-eight quarter-sections (7,680 acres) in this colony changed the situation. Thirty-one East European families, none of whom had encountered Canadian farming methods, were settled in the community between 1926 and 1928.[156] To provide housing and experience for the new farmers, the Oungre Farm Laborers' Hamlet was constructed. Each of the twenty-five-acre lots had a house, barn, and chicken house, and the land was sufficient to grow vegetables and feed cattle.[157] Harry Barish of Wapella, a graduate of Manitoba Agricultural College, was engaged by the ICA to teach new farmers the use of modern machinery.[158]

To install farmers permanently on the land the ICA developed a very liberal policy. Each farm of a half-section (320 acres) was provided with buildings, a minimum acreage cultivated, and other improvements made. The necessary equipment was supplied, along with seed and feed during the first year. These disbursements averaged $2,000 per newly-installed farmer in addition to the cost of land and improvements. Each candidate was given a trial period from one to three years. When the candidate paid off all the loans for the purchase of chattels, etc., at a modest interest rate of five percent, and was able to make a down payment of twenty percent on the cost of the farm, he was given an agreement for sale. The provincial Minister of Agriculture, who personally visited the Sonnenfeld Colony, had nothing but praise for this program.[159]

As a result of this ICA development the population of Sonnenfeld increased to 227, the highest in its history. The acreage under cultivation increased to almost 12,000. In 1929 the number

154. Belkin, pp. 162-163.
155. I. Hoffer, "Reminiscences," p. 31.
156. Feldman, p. 45.
157. Belkin, p. 163.
158. *Ibid.*, p. 165.
159. *Ibid.*, p. 164.

of horses was over 400, and of cattle almost 350. The annual crop yield amounted to 60,000 bushels of wheat, 29,000 bushels of oats, 18,000 bushels of barley, 1,200 bushels of rye, and 12,000 bushels of flax.[160] The Hoffer brothers' deaths, Mayer in 1952 and Israel in 1957, signalled the end of the colony. Today only one Jewish farmer remains in the district. Usher Berger, son of a founder, still farms thirteen quarter-sections (2,080 acres) of the colony's original land.

A modern times traveller-historian has written an epilogue to this colony:

> The Hoffer country even at its greenest is austere, lonely, in winter frightening in its unbroken grey-white immensity. A visit there is a salutary experience for those of us who are conditioned to associate the Jews with an urban society, and makes more readily comprehensible their astonishing achievement in our present century. For the qualities which enabled Jewish settlers to survive the hardships of homestead life on the prairies and to convert empty wastes into richly productive farms are precisely those which, exerted at a later time and in a different place, have helped to make for Jewry a fertile homeland of the deserts of Israel.[161]

---

160. Rosenberg, "Jews in Agriculture," p. 57.
161. Edward McCourt, *Saskatchewan*, The Traveller's Canada (Toronto: Macmillan of Canada, 1968, 1977), p. 40, reprinted by permission of Macmillan of Canada, a Division of Gage Publishing Limited.

THE JEWISH FARMERS OF WESTERN CANADA

By Cyril Edel Leonoff

Part III: Peak and Aftermath

By the end of the first decade of the twentieth century a sizable Jewish farm population was becoming rooted in the soil of Western Canada in five principal[162] and a number of smaller Jewish farm colonies or as independent farmers, singly or in small groups, scattered throughout the Northwest in Saskatchewan, Manitoba and Alberta.

Edenbridge, the last of the principal Jewish farm colonies in Saskatchewan, the most heroic and the most successful Jewish farm colony in Canada, started spontaneously. Three brothers, Louis, David, Sam and sister Fanny Vickar, along with a number of their fellow countrymen, had emigrated from Lithuania to South Africa during the Boer War.[163] The Vickars had been brought up in a rural village in the province of Vilna. Their father was employed in the winter as a log scaler and in the summer as overseer for sales of produce from three large farms belonging to a Polish landowner.[164]

In South Africa, these young people, Talmudic students and petty tradesmen, had a hard time getting established in Cape Town and neighboring towns. The Vickars bought a bakery and store in the town of Wynberg.[165] Eventually the Jewish people had adapted to the African conditions, got along fairly well financially, and made friends with the Boers, who were very hospitable. Nevertheless these Jews were not entirely happy in their adopted country. The conflict between the Boers and the British disturbed them. Coming from Northern Europe they were unaccustomed to the hot climate. Perhaps most of all, because of their rural upbringing, where they had been denied the privilege of owning land, they

---

162. Saskatchewan: Edenbridge (Brooksby-Gronlid-Ratner), Oxbow-Hirsch, Qu'Appelle (Lipton-Dysart-Cupar), Sonnenfeld (Oungre-Hoffer-Ratcliffe); Alberta: Rumsey-Trochu.
163. Louis Rosenberg, ed., "Zimbale to Edenbridge: The Autobiography of Samuel Vickar, a Pioneer Jewish Farmer in Canada," Canadian Jewish *Congress Bulletin*, Montreal, Parts I to V, January to May 1966.
164. *Ibid.*, pt. I, p. 2.
165. Harry Broudy, "An Essay: The Edenbridge Colony," 1952, pp. 59-70, Norman Rosenberg, comp., Norman Vickar, researcher, *Edenbridge the Memory Lives On: A History* (Melfort, 1980) p. 60; Vickar, pt. II, p. 6.

hoped some day "to gain real independence by becoming tillers of the soil," where they would be able "to derive their livelihood through . . . productive work."[166]

Near the end of 1904 the Vickars happened to read an article in an American Yiddish weekly newspaper. The author described his former life as a worker in a clothing factory where he had been in poor health. Advised to move out to the country, he had settled on a homestead in North Dakota. Having lived there for twelve years, he extolled the virtues of healthy farm life. But since there were no more free homesteads in North Dakota, he advised prospective settlers to look to Canada.[167]

The Vickars, their brother-in-law to be, Jacob Sweiden, and three Broudy brothers, Israel, Jack and Max, immediately took up this challenge. They wrote to the Department of the Interior in Ottawa, stating that "we are Jews who keep Saturday as our day of rest," asked whether they would be welcome in Canada. Six weeks later they received a reply that there was freedom of religion in Canada and everybody was welcome.[168]

These leaders organized a Colonization Society of about forty members whose objective was to move to land in Canada. The news spread to Cape Town where Rabbi Alfred P. Bender asked a delegation from the group to see him. He told them that he did not want young men to leave the community, promising that he would try to get them some land in South Africa.[169] But the most determined could not be dissuaded. Disposing of their belongings in 1906, eight families, comprised of twenty-two persons, made the final decision to go.[170]

Arriving in Winnipeg they sent two of their group, Herman Katzeff and Harry Wolfowitch (Wolff), to seek a suitable place for group settlement.[171] First offered land in the existing colonies of Hirsch and Lipton on the open plains, they chose instead to settle in the rainier timbered black-soil belt of North Central Saskatchewan. "These Jews of Vilna and Kovno . . . of little or no farm-

---

166. Broudy, p. 61.
167. Vickar, pt. II, p. 6.
168. *Ibid.*
169. *Ibid.*
170. Broudy, p. 61; Vickar, pt. II, p. 6.
171. *Edenbridge History,* pp. 92-94; 117-118; Broudy, p. 61.

ing experience . . . appreciated the value of running water for cattle and household purposes, and wood for fuel and building."[172]

Traveling north by rail the men arrived at a small village named Star City. Here they were advised that some fifteen miles north lay the Carrot River, where new land for homesteading had recently been surveyed. Hiring a team and wagon the newcomers arrived at the Carrot River which had to be forded as there was no

Beth Israel Synagogue, Edenbridge, Saskatchewan.
Constructed in 1908, it was used for sixty years.

bridge. In a remote spot one mile north of the river in thick bush and timber, Wolfowitch selected his homestead. Returning to Star City, they wired the rest of the group to come. Buying such essentials as axes, saws, nails and some food supplies, they constructed a log cabin twelve feet by twelve feet in size to accommodate the entire party.[173] This historic first building in the colony was later celebrated under the nickname "Edenbridge Hotel."

Sam Vickar, along with his brother David and younger sister

172. Vickar, pt. II, p. 8; Louis Rosenberg, "Jews in Agriculture in Western Canada," *The Israelite Daily Press*, 50th Anniversary of the Jews in the West, 1882-1932, Winnipeg, p. 57.
173. Vickar, pt. II, p. 8; Broudy, pp. 61-62.

Anna, has described their arrival at the "hotel" on July 26, 1906.

> The sun was beginning to set, and the mosquitoes were unbearable, so Eli Wolfowitch . . . started a fire and threw lots of green grass on it to make a smoke which would chase the mosquitoes away . . . We spent our first night upstairs in the so-called hotel, which had no doors to keep the big yellow mosquitoes out, and we could not sleep at all. . . . Friday afternoon . . . the sky began to cloud up and we heard thunder. Before sunset the women lit and blessed the Sabbath candles, and told us to come and eat supper. They served us rice soup on a rough table made of three poplar branches with a board from a grocery box nailed on top of them.[174]

At first the pioneers planned to build a rural village based on the model common in Eastern Europe. For this purpose they bought forty acres of land from the government at three dollars an acre on the north bank of the Carrot River. Five acres were allotted for a cemetery and the building of a synagogue. The other thirty-five acres were equally divided among the shareholders. The idea was that all would live in the village and each would go out from there to work his own land. This proved impractical in the bush country,[175] where wagons pulled by slow oxen over winding muddy trails were the only means of transportation, and was soon abandoned.

The first concern of the pioneers was to file for their homesteads at Melfort, the main town in the region, thirty miles southwest of the colony. The next tasks were to make some clearings in the forest, build a house, and break up some land for a garden.

> More accustomed to the pen than the double-bitted axe . . . in the dense poplar, jackpine and willow scrub . . . with their own blistered hands they won their little clearings acre by acre from the surrounding forest, and built their log houses and stables chinked with clay and coated with whitewash.[176]

For these purposes animals and equipment had to be procured. The Vickar brothers purchased a pair of oxen for $125 from a farmer and a wagon at Melfort. Before winter set in the men were

---

174. Vickar, pt. III, p. 2.
175. Broudy, pp. 67-68.
176. "Jews in Agriculture," p. 57.

able to erect four more log cabins and the first frame house built north of the Carrot River, at the Sweiden homestead, where the single Vickar brothers and sister also lived that first winter with their sister and brother-in-law. To withstand the minus fifty and sixty-degree winter weather and many severe blizzards, the log buildings were chinked with moss and the walls plastered inside and outside with clay and fibrous materials.[177]

When the inexperienced pioneers arrived in this untouched country that summer of 1906, they were fortunate to find two

A pioneer log cabin, Edenbridge,
Homestead of Rabbi Max Shallit.

young Englishmen, George Ellis and Isaac Brass, who had filed for homesteads the previous year. They had some farming experience and were handy in construction with a saw and hammer. They became very good friends with their Jewish neighbors and were adopted into the colony. When Sam and David Vickar and Jacob Sweiden hitched up the plough and oxen to break up their first plot for a garden, they met with failure. "So we called Isaac Brass and he . . . showed us how to make a start when ploughing. That

---

177. Broudy, pp. 63-65.

was when we found out that it was harder to be a farmer than a store clerk."[178]

At harvest time with their funds already depleted some of the men looked for work with the nearby farmers. They worked on threshing gangs and on farm chores from four o'clock in the morning until after dark. Being greenhorns they started out with fifteen dollars a month. The farmers were tolerant and the young Jewish men were willing to do hard work. They were eager to learn the rudiments of farming. After freeze-up they returned back home, having earned enough money to buy winter clothes and supplies.[179]

That winter was considered a period of prosperity. The colonists augmented their income by cutting and hauling wood to town, where a cord of good, dry wood would bring three dollars. The men would leave home by midnight, traveling with oxen, and arrive at Star City in the morning. One day the settlers looked out and saw a caravan of horses and wagons loaded with timber and supplies coming down the hill to the river. The government had sent out a construction crew to build a bridge over the Carrot River. Most of the men of the colony were employed as laborers on the bridge at the then favorable rate of two dollars a day. Sam Vickar and Jacob Sweiden each earned fifty-two dollars on the job.[180]

In 1907 the settlers applied to Ottawa and received approval for a local post office in the colony. Next came the question of a name.

> We all wanted to call it Jewish Bridge, but we thought that . . . the Postmaster General might not agree. We read through the list of names . . . in the Canadian Postal Guide, and found names beginning with Eden, so we made a quick and unanimous decision that the name of the new post office should be Edenbridge (Jews' Bridge), and that is how [the colony] got its name.

David Vickar became the first postmaster, for which the government paid thirty-five dollars a year to attend to the duties two days a week. He received an additional one hundred dollars per year to haul the mail to and from Star City. For the post office

---

178. *Edenbridge History*, pp. 71-75; Broudy, p. 64; Vickar, pt. III, pp. 2, 4.
179. *Ibid.*, pt. III, p. 4; Broudy, pp. 63-64.
180. Vickar, pt. IV, p. 6.

they built a "shack" across the road from the Sweiden house.[181]

The forest was so thick, the trails between homesteads nebulous, and the landmarks few so the settler had to take great care not to lose his way even on his own homestead. One evening Jack Broudy went into the bush to find his cow and oxen. The animals came home on their own but Jack was lost. His neighbors searched for him all the next day. When they got back that afternoon Jack

Jack and Fanny (Vickar) Sweiden house
at Edenbridge, built in 1906.

was already home. The weather had cleared, he had found the river and followed it back to the bridge.

The transition of a homesteader to a farmer at Edenbridge was a slow and tedious process. Little by little the pioneers wrested their farms from the forest. In 1907 Isaac Brass broke five acres of new land and the Vickar family eight acres.[182] In August 1908 they bought the first binder in the Jewish settlement. That fall they had their first crop of oats, and hired a little portable steam

181. *Ibid.*
182. *Ibid.*

thresher. In 1910 ten of the Jewish farmers got together and bought a large second-hand threshing machine for $1,000.[183]

After the settlers had looked after their own means of survival, they had to attend to the necessary communal needs of a Jewish community.

> Rosh Hashanah was approaching, and we had to make preparations. The first problem was to obtain a *Sefer Torah*. We decided to write to . . . Winnipeg, and ask . . . to borrow one and send it to us in Star City, and we would return it after the High Holy Days. . . . But to our surprise we received a telegram . . . that they wanted forty dollars for the loan . . . so we had to collect . . . and wire the money . . . for the *Sefer Torah*, which was shipped to us by express. . . . We had a *minyon* and the services were held in Sweiden's house.[184]

The cemetery was registered in 1906, and the first interment was in 1907. Two years later the settlers pooled their resourcs and built a simple wooden synagogue. Beth Israel Synagogue served the community for sixty years, from its opening on Rosh Hashanah 1908 until its official closing in October, 1968 when a *minyon* could no longer be maintained.[185]

The colony needed a religious leader, so they advertised in a Winnipeg Jewish newspaper. Rabbi Max Shallit responded. He took up a homestead and assumed the life of a pioneer in the colony. He also served as *schochet* and Jewish teacher. His wife and three small children joined him in the colony. With his salary of fifteen dollars a month from the community, he was considered quite well-to-do. The Shallit family were well liked in the community and popular with the gentile neighbors, particularly the Ukrainians, for whom he acted as an English correspondent.[186] Before a community hall was erected the Shallit home was the stopping place where "one found the spirit of Edenbridge." Mrs. Shallit was "a clever woman who understood that every mile of travel increases the appetite and who had already prepared."[187]

To create a viable Jewish community they needed more Jew-

---

183. *Ibid.*, p. 8.
184. *Ibid.*, pt. III, p. 4.
185. *Edenbridge History*, p. 47.
186. Broudy, p. 67.
187. Mike Usiskin, *From Oxen to Tractors: Reminiscences of a Jewish Farm Pioneer* (Toronto, 1945), translated from the Yiddish by A. I. Bereskin (Regina, Archives of Saskatchewan, 1953-1954), p. 56.

ish pioneers. Louis Vickar, "who was quite handy with a pen," wrote a series of articles for the newspaper *Varheit* of New York. He wrote optimistically about the Edenbridge Colony. These articles appealed to a number of people in the United States, and as a result the population soon increased with the addition of such men as brothers Frank and Max Gordon, Philip Gordon (no relation), and their families.[188] More far-reaching was another migration of a group of young men, born in Eastern Europe, who were laboring in the sweat shops of Whitechapel in London.

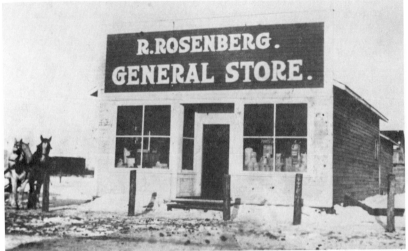

First country store at Edenbridge was established in 1910 by Raphael and Anna (Vickar) Rosenberg. From 1920 to 1946 they operated this store in the hamlet of Brooksby.

Through an article appearing in a newspaper, these laborers learned of the existence of Edenbridge and "grasped at the opportunity." They looked for someone in London who might give them more information and located Mrs. Shallit's brother. Rabbi Shallit then wrote to them from Edenbridge:

> Flee from the London fogs . . . flee from the dismal tenements and the bosses who live on your blood and sweat. . . . Come to us. The air here is pleasant and the place is still and restful. . . . The forest here is so huge that one can expand as the heaven desires. One lives on ones own resources. Our com-

---

188. Broudy, p. 67; *Edenbridge History*, pp. 89-91.

munity will welcome you with open arms. Come complete our
colony — we need your extra energies.[189]

Mike Usiskin, a furrier by trade in London, the chronicler of
these events, has left us a vivid description of pioneer life in the
colony.

> From the turmoil of London to the deathly silence of the
> forests . . . what devilish power could make me leave London
> and what magnetic attraction could keep me in Edenbridge
> for thirty-three years? The call of the land pulled us strongly.
> . . . We were young and strong and afraid not of hard work.
> Also a small newspaper clipping . . . sent from Edenbridge
> of a dramatic play which they performed . . . convinced me
> that the Edenbridge colonists were quite cultured and were
> concerned about spiritual matters, even though settled in the
> midst of the forest.[190]

The first expedition left London for Canada in May 1910
and a second in May 1911, including several families such as Dave
and Mike Usiskin, Isy Segal, Isaac Cohen, the four Springman
brothers, Alex, Barney, Joseph and Reuben, and the Nathan Freedman family.[191] Branches of the latter two families today yet farm
the soil of Edenbridge. Mike Usiskin described his arrival at the
colony in 1911:

> Coming to the last station where the conductor called
> "Star City" I was to get off. I was alone [the rest of the party
> had been held up in Quebec]. The man I saw at first . . . was
> wearing . . . muddy overalls. On his head a fur cap with ear-
> laps and a fur jacket on his shoulders. . . . I envied him his
> warm dress compared to mine, in my summer clothes and teeth
> chattering from the cold. . . .
>
> No one need envy our trip home . . . without a sign of a
> road between heavy woods and large swamps . . . when sudden-
> ly the wind changed and we had a snowstorm on the 26th of
> May. Mud holes deeper than our wheels. The horses could
> hardly pull themselves out and we were spattered from head to
> toe, lying in a bare wagon box, without a bit of hay or straw,
> as we tried to sleep. . . . Our ribs were sore all night from the
> jostling of the wagon. . . .
>
> Nowhere did they stop until they came to the house of the
> first Jewish farmer. We heard a hail "Fellow Israelites, come
> in". . . . My hand was grasped by another almost twice as big,

---

189. Usiskin, p. 9.
190. *Ibid.*, pp. 1, 9, 11-12.
191. *Ibid.*, pp. 11, 13; *Edenbridge History*, pp. 98-101, 88-89.

and so calloused and hard and yet warm, with a friendly smile. . . . And so this is Dave Usiskin's brother from London. We have long waited for you. Who else came with you? We need many more Jews here, sturdy ones, not delicate ones, who are not frightened by petty difficulties. We have such colossal labour — the swamps to drain, the roads to improve, so that we can pass freely and enjoy the fruits of our pioneer life.

Charles Brotman and sons, with a steam thresher,
Brandon, Manitoba, 1913.

I wonder as to their living accommodation. Where is the house? I see before me what appears to be a large box, about big enough for a couple of dozen geese. And here in that . . . box there lived a family with children. . . . I overheard this conversation: "Rosa climb out of bed and let some fellow Israelite, weary from travel, sleep. We shall rest tomorrow," and she answered: "Husband, help unharness and tell them to come into the house and I will have tea and a bite to eat ready for them."[192]

Soon after arrival at this brother's "palace" (shack), Usiskin went alone to the post office, six miles away, for the mail.

Without any sign of a road . . . my brother . . . who came here a year earlier . . . gave me various landmarks to follow..

192. Usiskin, pp. 14, 16-18.

Every mile under normal conditions requires three miles to skirt the swamps. . . . Most of the colonists sing at their work and this and the sound of wood chopping is used by travellers to avoid becoming lost. True, the forests were inhabited — the birds singing in the sun. . . . The frogs in the swamps croaked continuously. . . . You may meet large animals with mighty horns. These are moose who will not bother you if you ignore them. . . . And so I went from one neighbor to another, from one swamp to another, jumping over puddles and walking over fallen logs to avoid the wet grass . . . already wet to the waste — until I yearned for a street car, or even a team of oxen. My city shoes were in tatters but, as I could not discard them, I made strips of my handkerchiefs and bound the soles to the uppers.[193]

The post office was a tiny building about the size of a bedroom. There was a compartment for the mail sacks and correspondence, and a larger space for the public who came to wait for the mail. A box stove was the center of attraction, and people huddled around it and conversed like geese.[194]

On the lifestyle of the homesteader Usiskin wrote:

When could we have dreamt to own such vast lands — imagine 160 acres. . . . Nature is still new and the thousand year old forests are so dense that sunlight barely comes through. . . . We have plenty of work here but we work for ourselves. . . .

Where can you find a place like this where we are all alike? We are all poor dressed in patched overalls, we smoke cheap tobacco, we are all one family, without false ideas, no wealthy classes at present but of the future let God decide. . . . The homes are . . . without light or water similar to the wild Indians. . . . True we are struggling a little too hard for our bread but we hope that in time we shall have broad fields of wheat, that all will be fruitful and we will have all we need. . . . Thus we lived in extreme poverty but without worry which was the sweetening of our life where we lived without locks to our doors. . . .

But this thought was uppermost — we are young and strong and full of courage. . . . Furthermore we are not here alone. . . . We felt that individually our strength was puny — one man can lift only so much and two together can do far more. . . . These here are our brethren. . . . True we are separated from one another and can not operate as a collective . . .

---

193. *Ibid.*, pp. 19-20, 90.
194. *Ibid.*, p. 24.

but we can cooperate among ourselves in other ways. . . . So we work . . . on each farm so as to prove it up. . . . Here we were young Jewish men . . . stripped to the waist with sun burnt hide and hardy muscles . . . with calloused hands used to the 6 pound double bitted axe. . . . The forest trembled with fright that little men with such a spirit could conquer such a mighty forest.[195]

Jack Pressman with a calf, New Hirsch Colony, Manitoba, c. 1922.

The men were away from home days at a time. The women had to do the men's work at home, such as feeding the stock, milking, and cleaning out the barns. Bringing in the wood to heat the flimsy houses was quite a chore. In addition the women had to patch the clothes which men wore out quickly, especially in chop-

195. *Ibid.*, pp. 36, 38, 48, 67, 68, 77, 78, 80.

ping trees. There was little money with which to buy new clothes.[196] The women were isolated on the homesteads.

> We are cut off from the world. . . . There is not a shop to buy anything — not even a bit of coal oil.. . . . Often the mother has little food to pack in the lunch box for her children. . . . The children must go four miles or more to school through the forests, without [adequate] shoes.[197]

At first the settlers relied on their own limited resources. One day an Edenbridge farmer travelled to Winnipeg to buy horses. To raise enough money he had to pawn his watch and his wife's bracelet. It was then that he learned of Baron de Hirsch and the Jewish Colonization Association (ICA).[198] The Edenbridge Jewish Co-operative Credit Union was formed in 1910. The ICA loaned the Union $1,000, which was repaid as it became self-sustaining. Interest rates were 8%, corresponding to bank rates. The Union was dissolved as settlers became self-supporting.[199]

In November 1912 the Rural Municipality of Willow Creek, in which the colony was located, was created. David Vickar served for twenty-two years as reeve (mayor), and Sam Vickar was reeve for ten years. In recent years Charles Vickar, a son of David, has been reeve. In January 1911 the settlers petitioned the Minister of Education requesting the formation of a public school district. The Edenbridge School No. 2930 was officially opened for classes during the fall term of 1913, with Raphael Rosenberg first chairman of the school board. Eventually two public schools served the settlement.[200]

Small groups of immigrants continued to arrive, bringing the community's population to a high of some fifty families in the early 1920s. By this time 7,500 acres were under cultivation.[201] Most of the settlers established their farm sites along the range line commencing at the Jack Broudy farm, four miles north of Star City, and continuing on twenty miles north to the Freedman

196. *Ibid.*, p. 61.
197. *Ibid.*, p. 31.
198. Abraham J. Arnold, "The Edenbridge Story," *The Western Jewish News,* Winnipeg, June 17, 1976, p. 3.
199. *R.M. of Willow Creek No. 458: Jubilee Year 1912-1962* (Melfort: Melfort Journal Press, 1962), p. 58.
200. *Ibid.*, pp. 67, 85, 87; *Edenbridge History*, pp. 24-25; Broudy, p. 70.
201. Simon Belkin, *Through Narrow Gates* (Montreal, 1966), p. 80.

and I. Taback farms. Others established along the east-west township line.[202]

In the 1920s, when the railways came through to the colony, the hamlets of Brooksby, Gronlid, and Ratner (named after the Jacob Ratner family) were established. They contained Jewish-owned general stores, garages, implement businesses, and a small hotel. Jewish farmers and merchants took an active part in the agricultural and community life of the neighborhood. In 1908 Louis Vickar became the first Justice of the Peace in the Edenbridge district. Jewish men served as reeves, secretary-treasurers, and councillors of the rural municipality, postmasters, members of the public school and hospital boards, and took an active part in farmers' cooperative societies.[203] Norman Vickar, a native son

Charles and Ethel Waterman family and friends,
Trochu Colony, Alberta, 1915.

---

202. *Edenbridge History*, p. 17.
203. *Willow Creek*, pp. 62-63, 65, 53-58, 83-94; *Edenbridge History*, pp. 95-96.

of the colony, has represented the constituency as a member of the Saskatchewan Legislature.

As the colony expanded, the settlers built a community hall along the township line, which became the focal center for the neighborhood. Here were held dances and the annual sports days. They established a library with Yiddish and English books, had one and at times two, Jewish teachers instructing Hebrew and Yiddish classes. There was a dramatic society, a debating team, a children's educational club, a Judaen club, and a hectographed Jewish and English periodical that appeared at irregular intervals. Thus Edenbridge became, in microcosm, a total Jewish community usually found only in large urban centers.[204]

In July 1931 the community celebrated its silver anniversary. A parade marshaled at the Edenbridge Hall, headed by a team of oxen pulling a farm wagon carrying the original 1906 pioneers, set out for the synagogue, four miles distant. The parade passed over improved roads, by homes built of sawn lumber and fields of waving grain, which had replaced the log cabins and forest of yesteryear. Enroute a stop was made at a deteriorated log building, identified by a huge banner as the "Edenbridge Hotel." At the synagogue a ceremony was held with David Vickar, president of the Jewish community, master of ceremonies. Members of the provincial and federal governments were platform guests. The day concluded with a picnic and sports events.[205]

Saturday, June 26, 1976, on the seventieth anniversary of the establishment of the community, a homecoming was held for descendants of Edenbridge Colony from all over the continent. A Hebrew service was conducted in the beautifully preserved and restored synagogue. This was followed by a banquet attended by the Premier of the province, at which the synagogue, cemetery and the original forty acres of land of the colony were dedicated as a Province of Saskatchewan historic site.[206] By this time only four Jewish families were still farming the land of Edenbridge. Edenbridge Colony has been aptly eulogized by a contemporary ob-

---

204. *Edenbridge History,* p. 17; Broudy, p. 69; "Edenbridge Story."
205. *Edenbridge History,* pp. 41-42.
206. *Ibid.,* pp. 53-55.

server as a "monument to the courage, enterprise and adaptability of the Jew."[207]

Manitoba was established as a province in 1870. When Jewish landseekers arrived, good farm land in blocks was generally unavailable. The Jewish farmers tended to settle in small groups or as individuals. The largest groups were at Bender Hamlet (Narcisse), New Hirsch (Camper), Birds Hill, and Pine Ridge.[208]

One of the unique farm settlements in Canada was Bender Hamlet, founded in 1902 as a planned agricultural village. It survived for a quarter century. It was a replica of a medieval East European *Strassendorf* — a one-street village with the houses and their lots on one side, fields on the other.

Jacob Bender came from a *shtetl* and landed in Winnipeg at the turn of the century. He is variously described as an "owner of a group of general stores," a "speculator," and a "land agent." In search of land in February 1902, Bender traveled thirty miles northwest of Winnipeg to the end of the road at the town of Teulon in the interlake region. Beyond this was the Colonization Road, a track through unpopulated, uncleared bush and sloughs, reliable only after freezeup in the winter. Being from the Ukraine, where wood was a coveted commodity, he saw an economic potential in harvesting the "forest." In fact most of the prime spruce and tamarack timber, except for isolated stands, had been razed by a great fire in the 1870s and most of the second growth cover was of little economic value. He purchased a site some thirty miles northwest along the trail and sixty miles from Winnipeg.

Bender made a rapid recruitment trip to England and Eastern Europe and with the promise of land and riches had no trouble in recruiting eighteen families who settled on the land between 1902 and 1904. Most came from Russia with some from England and elsewhere. They were merchants, tailors, etc., and there were a couple of gardeners with a passing knowledge of farming.

The settlers received a concession from the government to divide Bender's quarter-section of land into nineteen equal strips one-half mile deep (about eight and one-half acres each). One lot

207. "Jews in Agriculture," p. 56.
208. Belkin, p. 82.

was used for the synagogue and cemetery. They began clearing the lots and building their homes facing north along the section line on a street half a mile long. Substantial houses were erected on lime-stone basements. Each family also obtained a homestead quarter-section around the village.

In December 1912 the Canadian Northern Railway pushed through to the colony. The station, two miles west of the hamlet, was named Narcisse after Narcisse Leven, president of the ICA. With the coming of the railway the farmers were able to ship their grain, beef and dairy products to market in Winnipeg. In the peak year of 1915 there were thirty-nine Jewish families and 182 people in the hamlet and surrounding district. By 1917 there were 6,197 acres owned and clear assets of $82,059. That year the settlers built the Narcisse Co-operative Creamery and Cheese Factory. The colony "exuded vitality and thrived on optimism." Communal life consisted of shul (synagogue) every Saturday, a public school, Hebrew lessons after conventional school, parties, picnics and games.[209]

The colony, however, had inherent problems. The fall in cattle prices after World War I dealt a heavy economic blow. Bender had chosen poor farmland. The land was simultaneously too wet and too dry. The sand ridges wouldn't retain water and the clay bottoms wouldn't drain. Therefore the crops were always spotty.[210]

The village plan did not work out successfully under Canadian conditions. Living in close proximity, there was the usual gossiping and quarrels among neighbors. In the days where motive power was by animals it proved uneconomical to live up to five miles from the homestead and commute each day. Some of the farmers eventually moved onto their homesteads and erected buildings thereon.[211]

The final problem of the community was socio-cultural. The colony on the one hand was too far removed from the city to enjoy the fruits of the vibrant Jewish communal life of Winnipeg. On the

209. Ted Allan, "New Jerusalem Just a Memory: Pioneering Jews Struggled Hard in Unique Bender Hamlet Venture," *Winnipeg Free Press*, December 10, 1980, based on interview with Jack Lavitt, son of pioneer families. Material also obtained by the writer from a descendant, Joseph Lavitt.
210. "Jews in Agriculture," p. 56; Allan, *loc. cit.*
211. "Jews in Agriculture," p. 56.

other hand it was too close, which allowed a disadvantageous comparison between life on the farm and the relative affluence and other attractions of the city. Education terminated at grade eight. Inevitably, when the children started to grow up, they visited Winnipeg and came back to the colony dissatisfied. Once the young people started to leave the end of the colony was pre-ordained.

After three years of torrential spring rains in 1924-1926, which washed out the crops, the last of the colonists departed in 1927. Because of the poor soil and bad economic conditions, neighboring Ukrainian and Scandinavian settlements were also entirely deserted.[212]

The New Hirsch Colony at Camper was founded in 1911 in the interlake region forty miles northwest of Bender Hamlet. Established by some twenty families from Winnipeg who had originally farmed in the Ukraine, it flourished for several years with cattle raising and dairying. However, the colony suffered similar poor soil and economic conditions as Bender Hamlet and was abandoned in 1924. Neither of these colonies were founded with the advice of the ICA, but both subsequently received assistance from that organization, too late, when difficult economic conditions developed. Many of the New Hirsch farmers relocated closer to the city of Winnipeg where they engaged in dairy farming.[213]

The most successful groups of Jewish farmers in Manitoba were those who established on the outskirts or within commuting distance of Winnipeg at Birds Hill, Pine Ridge, Tanscona, Lorette, Ste Anne, Rosenfeld, Rosser, Kildonan and Gimli. Such farmers were less isolated, able to give to their children a Jewish education, and to join their city relatives or friends during the major festivals and holy days. Settlements at Birds Hill, Pine Ridge and West Kildonan were large enough to build their own synagogues. For more than two decades these Jewish farmers succeeded in dairy-farming, poultry-raising, and truck-farming. But their numbers were greatly reduced by the ravages of the depression in the 1930s.[214] The Jewish dairy farmers of West Kildonan provided a large portion of Winnipeg's milk supplies until taken over by housing subdivisions after World War II.

---

212. Allan and Joseph Lavitt; "Jews in Agriculture," p. 56.
213. *Ibid.,* p. 58.
214. Arthur A. Chiel, *The Jews in Manitoba* (Toronto, 1961), p. 56.

The Rosser settlement was established in 1934 as a depression relief project to bring farmers back to the land. It was composed of nine families. The colony consisted of a street of houses on ten-acre lots, with outlying fields of 960 acres. The predominant family of this settlement is that of pioneer Harry Pressman, who originally farmed at New Hirsch before relocating to Rosser. Today this land is farmed by Pressman's son Morris, wife Minnie (Zeitlin), and their two sons, Sol and Aaron, the third generation of farmers in the family. Minnie's father Aaron Zeitlin was a pioneer farmer and Jewish teacher at the Hirsch and Lipton colonies.[215]

Alberta is the most westerly of Canada's prairie provinces. Jewish colonization here was generally later than in Manitoba and Saskatchewan.

A few Jews settled in Alberta in the 1890s. Among them were some individuals and small groups of farmers and ranchers. The first High Holy Day services in Alberta took place in 1894 in the old Masonic Hall of the largest city, Calgary. The congregation was composed of "two residents of Calgary, two from Edmonton, five commercial travelers, and a farmer from near Lacombe."[216]

The earliest Jewish farm colonies of Alberta were founded near the villages of Trochu and Rumsey in the Red Deer River valley about 120 miles northeast of Calgary. Most of the settlers were from the Ukraine and Russia. Trochu was on the more accessible west bank of the river, and was closer to rail connection. On the east bank, where Rumsey was located, there was no railway into the district until 1911.[217] The early settlers had to walk or ride into the homesteads from the towns of Olds or Innisfail west of the river for distances of up to sixty miles, swim, or at low water, ford the river. The trip from Calgary took nearly a week by horse team. A ferry crossing was in service between 1907 and 1925.[218]

The first Trochu settlers arrived by the year 1905 or earlier.

---

215. The writer visited this farm and interviewed Morris and Minnie Pressman on June 8, 1979.
216. Rosenberg, *Canada's Jews: A Social and Economic Study of the Jews in Canada* (Montreal, 1939), p. 147.
217. *Pioneer Days: History of Rumsey and District*, Centennial Year, 1967, p. 5.
218. *Pioneer Days; Book Two* (Rumsey, 1982), p. 763.

The principal Jewish families there were brothers Charles and Max Waterman, Morris Katzin, Leib Cramer and Max Silver.[219] The colony was located eight to ten miles southeast of Trochu. The area east of the river was opened for homesteading in 1905-1906.

Two brothers, Raphael and Louis Gurevitch, left Russia for the new world in 1902 after serving in the Russian army. Arriving in Eastern Canada, they met with a compatriot Elias Sengaus. The three worked as laborers on construction projects. Working their way west, the young men "robust, healthy, adventurous and above all ambitious" worked in a lumber camp in Sault Ste Marie. But, when the camp burned down they boarded a train going west to Calgary in the year 1904 to go homesteading.

Four days travel by horse and wagon over bald prairie and grass land brought them into a parkland on the east bank of the Red Deer River "where grass was up to a horse's belly," lakes and sloughs were "fresh and productive with wild life and game," and "wild flowers were everywhere." The three companions spent the first years together "sharing a sod shack and learning to become farmers the hard way."

Returning to Calgary from this expedition the news spread like wildfire among the many Jewish newcomers who had fled from Russia at the time of the Russo-Japanese War. About seventy-five men filed for homesteads. Almost no one had previous farming experience, but this did not matter to them. Here was a chance to own land, a privilege they had been denied in their homelands. Thus "almost overnight" a Jewish colony formed.[220] The Jewish farmers of Rumsey Colony settled within a radius of eight miles from the village.

The public school districts were established in the early years. Tolman School No. 2204, built in 1908, four and one-half miles west of Rumsey in the heart of the Jewish district, had some thirty pupils most of whom were Jewish. Following school hours Jewish children attended classes of instruction in Hebrew and Yiddish taught by teachers hired by the Jewish community, several of whom served over the years. The most noteworthy was Elias Sengaus

---

219. Freda (Waterman) Levy, Vancouver, interview, by the writer, May 4, 1983.
220. *Pioneer Days II*, pp. 555-557.

who served as a teacher, *mohel* (circumciser), and *schochet*, traveling to remote farms to do so until his death in 1956.[221]

In 1917, "the desire to preserve a little of their own culture and customs" motivated the building of a synagogue near the Tolman School. This was a community effort, labor being volunteered and funds donated. The principal carpenters were J. Cohen and "Big John" Gelfond. During the High Holy Days Jewish farmers and storekeepers converged from a twenty mile radius with over sixty families and filled the synagogue to capacity. The Trochu group was directly across (west of) the river from the Rumsey settlers. However, as the ferry was the only means of crossing in the years that it operated, the Trochu settlers were generally isolated from the others. They held their own religious services and met socially in private homes.[222]

The Jewish community of Rumsey maintained a warm social life centered around the synagogue. Raphael Gurevitch had a portable gramaphone "with about fifty records . . . to supply the two-step or waltz music." Samuel Davis, a Jewish farmer, was a dance teacher. Ben Gurevitch "swung a fine fiddle" in demand for parties and weddings both Jewish and gentile. He was talented enough to later play in the Calgary Symphony Orchestra. Sport was not overlooked. The Rumsey Jewish baseball team was good enough to travel to Calgary and win. Harold Raskin won the middleweight boxing championship at the University of Alberta. Tom Sengaus was a "top-notch" high school football player, and won a wrestling championship at Calgary Tech.[223]

The Rumsey and Trochu colonies were fortunate in establishing on very fertile land, having a much higher precipitation than the colonies in the drybelt of Saskatchewan, and were favored with bountiful crops. The major problem was frequent hail storms which are peculiar to the region, and sometimes play havoc with the crops. The decade 1910-1920 was fruitful. By this time the Jewish population in the Rumsey-Trochu district was 238, and 10,000 acres were under cultivation. They were then the wealthiest Jewish colonies in Canada. But some of the farmers at the time of inflated

221. *Ibid.*, pp. 539-542, 582, 602.
222. *Pioneer Days I*, pp. 10-11; Freda (Waterman) Levy.
223. *Pioneer Days II*, pp. 602-603.

land values had obtained large mortgage loans and found themselves in a hopeless position during the difficult economic period after World War I. This caused many abandonments.[224] Started independently, the colonies were later assisted by the ICA. Those who remained for many years became among the most affluent of all the Jewish farmers in Canada.

In addition to their farming chores the Jewish farmers practiced their trades that they brought with them from the old country. These skills were a considerable asset to the general community. J. Cohen, the carpenter, built several homes in the district. Jacob Wofson was a blacksmith, and "his left-handed power pounded out many a plow share." M. Kurtzberg was a leather and harness maker. Rudolph Engle was a watchmaker who was involved in construction of the Calgary City Hall clock, which today is still a landmark in that city. Harry Baron opened a shoe cobbler shop in Rumsey.[225]

The last Jewish farmer, Jack Cramer, left the Trochu district in the 1960s. A number of the pioneer Jewish families of Rumsey Colony established long-time farming dynasties which have endured for three-quarters of a century. When the writer visited the Tolman district in September 1974 we found that 7,600 acres were being farmed by families of the pioneers including the Sam Raskin family (also encompassing the Gurevitch farms), Ben, Tom and William Sengaus, Harry and Sam Silberstein.[226] Until their retirement in 1979, Fred Horodezky and his wife Fannie (Applebaum) operated the beautiful 2-F Bar Ranch, thirty miles north of Pincher Creek "where his hand picked herd brings . . . the highest prices because of their quality." Feted on their fifty-fifth wedding anniversary in 1976, as reported in the press: "Mr. Horodezky is probably the only rancher in Southern Alberta who *davens* (prays) three times a day and his spouse the only wife of a Jewish rancher who keeps a strictly kosher home."[227] Sam Rosenthal, son of pioneer William Rosenthal, today operates three farms and ranches near Calgary, Stavely and Wetaskiwin.

224. Belkin, p. 82; "Jews in Agriculture," p. 57; *Pioneer Days I*, p. 10; *Pioneer Days II*, p. 582.
225. *Ibid., pp.* 603, 375, 692-699.
226. *Ibid.,* pp. 579, 581-585, 585-587.
227. *Ibid.,* pp. 62-63; *The Jewish Western Bulletin*, Vancouver, April 1, 1976, p. 16.

In 1910 the farm settlements of Montefiore (Sibbald) and Eyre (Alsask) came into being astride the Alberta-Saskatchewan border, founded by groups of Jews some of whom had originally farmed in North Dakota and Montana. Although good farmers they unfortunately chose light, drought-stricken windblown lands. They started on their own, and when the ICA finally came to the rescue their position was hopeless. However, six Jewish farmers clung to the district until World War II. Many of the pioneer Jewish farmers of these settlements returned to the United States where they engaged in poultry farming in the Petaluma district of California.[228]

Another major Jewish rancher of note in Southeast Alberta has been Harry Veiner, who also served from 1959 to 1967 as Mayor of Medicine Hat, a city of only twenty Jewish families.

British Columbia is a mountainous province and generally not a major agricultural producer. Because of transportation difficulties in mountain terrain, much of the province has been sparsely populated and isolated from markets. However, the river valleys are fertile. The sunny interior valleys produce commercial apple and fruit crops of world renown. The central interior plateau "Cariboo" region is famous for its huge ranches. The lower Fraser River Valley, which stretches from the port of Vancouver to 100 miles inland, is noted for its dairy and poultry farms and market gardens.

Jewish people have not taken up farming in British Columbia in communities as they have in the prairie provinces. Through much of its history British Columbia has been a frontier province inhabited by rugged individualists. There have been a number of isolated Jewish farmers and ranchers who have fitted this mold. The great diversity of these figures is shown in the following examples.

Native-born William B. Sylvester was the oldest son of Frank Sylvester, the first recorded Jew to arrive in Victoria, B.C., in July 1858, and Cecelia (Davies) Sylvester. In the late nineteenth century Bill Sylvester operated the Sylvester Feed Company in Victoria, and owned the Gap Ranch, Shawnigan Lake, Vancouver

228. *Canada's Jews*, p. 223.

Island. His brothers Clarence and Jesse were also partners in the business and in the early stages their father Frank was accountant for the firm. They were "nice kindly men," and "if they had any weakness it was in their willingness to sit down and yarn . . . if anyone started a conversation which involved hunting, fishing, [or] farming . . ."[229] The company became a well established feed and milling business, occupying a three-story brick building in downtown Victoria, and at one time being worth about $200,000. It operated until Bill's death in 1931.[230]

Jacob Wasserman was an itinerant farmer-rabbi, one of the earliest in the Canadian west. A scholarly, gentlemanly person, his East European training and natural aptitude was for the pulpit. However, he really didn't enjoy being a rabbi and strongly pursued his efforts to be a farmer. Prior to the official founding of a congregation in Regina, Wasserman acted as *mohel* and *schochet* for that community.[231]

About 1896 Wasserman, a married man with eight children, settled at Oxbow where he farmed 395 acres. There he was "reader" of the Hebrew congregation. Three bad crop years at Oxbow and high interest rates put him in debt. In 1903 he bought a farm at Armstrong, B.C. where "the farming was very rough." He moved to Naramata in the Southern Okanagan Valley where he had a fruit farm for ten years. There Wasserman fell ill with a heart condition and died in 1914.[232]

Isidor Director was born in 1885 on the border of Germany and Poland. He came to America at the age of seventeen. Director and his Montreal-born wife Hannah spent fourteen years in Northern British Columbia at the port of Prince Rupert and at the interior center of Prince George, where they were pioneers in the formative years of these cities. Both talented people, the Directors'

229. A. J. Helmcken, "Main Street Victoria 1908: The Fabulous 700 Block," *The Daily Colonist*, Victoria, April 23, 1967, p. 4.
230. Elise Dorothy Menkus Reed, "The Story of the Sylvester Family," manuscript, August 1966, p. 8.
231. Arnold, "The First Rabbis in Saskatchewan," *The Western Jewish News,* October 2, 1980, p. 3; Maxwell Cohen, Q. C. (grandson), Ottawa, to the writer, August 21, October 9, 1979; Dept. of the Interior, Homestead Records, Saskatchewan Archives, Saskatoon; Arthur D. Hart, ed., *The Jew in Canada* (Toronto and Montreal, 1926), p. 155.
232. "First Rabbis;" *Jew in Canada*, p. 168; Cohen, to the writer; Maggie (Wasserman) Brownstone (daughter), interview, by the writer, March 26, 1969.

activities were varied. In 1908 Isidor Director and Maurice B. Cohen started out as squatters, established the first Jewish business in Prince Rupert, a clothing store. Hannah Director was a violinist in the Prince Rupert Symphony Orchestra and acted in dramatics.[233]

Moving to Prince George in 1913, the Director family took up a homestead twenty-two miles south of town on the Fraser River. With their three young children they endured primitive conditions, living in a log house with a packed dirt floor. She taught the children by correspondence. In 1917 Hannah Director became chairman of the Board of School Trustees in Prince George, the first Jewish woman elected to public office in Canada.[234] Moving back to Prince Rupert after the war, he became a longshoreman. The Directors moved to Vancouver in 1922 and opened a print shop. Here they published, in 1925, the first Anglo-Jewish newspaper in British Columbia. They became leading members of the Vancouver community. In long and fruitful lifetimes, through sixty-four years of marriage, Isidor and Hannah Director "exemplified the pioneer spirit" and in 1961 received an award as "outstanding citizens."[235]

Philip Adelberg, adventurer and world traveller, born in Lithuania, went to South Africa before the turn of the century, where he did some trekking and farming. During the Boer War he fought on the side of the Boers against the British. After the war he went to South America, spending six years in Argentina where he was in the horse and cattle business. Coming to Calgary, he worked as an engineer-builder of streets and housing. Here he married Lottie Ratchesky, daughter of a pioneer Jewish homesteading family from Lithuania.

In 1913 Adelberg, with his wife and two young children, organized and led the one Jewish and twelve Irish-Catholic families to homestead in the Peace River Block on the Alberta-British Columbia boundary, where the last frontier for wheat farming in the Northwest was being opened for homesteading. Since there were no roads or bridges into the area, they travelled by sleigh train. The party spent two winters travelling from Calgary over

---

233. Leonoff, Pioneers, *Pedlars, and Prayer Shawls: The Jewish Communities in British Columbia and the Yukon* (Victoria, 1978), pp. 43, 209.
234. *Ibid.*, p. 68.
235. *Ibid.*, pp. 143-145, 209-210.

the frozen Athabaska River and Lesser Slave Lake to reach their destination near Dawson Creek. Lottie Adelberg was a true pioneer woman. While her husband was engaged in surveying the road out to Prince Rupert for a year, she worked the homestead herself, ploughing and driving the team of horses. She *koshered* the wild meat (moose and venison). The gentile women of the district started to copy her in this process. It took the wild tang out of the meat. Ownership of the farm remained in the Adelberg family until the mid-1960s.[236]

Through the years about a dozen Jewish farm families are known to have established in the Fraser Valley as dairy and cattle farmers, poultry raisers and market gardeners, illustrated in the following examples. There have also been a number of Jewish cattle dealers, meat packers, fruit and vegetable wholesalers in the Vancouver area.

Sam and Anne Sussel left Germany in 1935 when they were prevented from practicing their professions of law and pediatrics, respectively. In 1941 they settled on the land in Chilliwack, B.C. Sam Sussel and his wife knew little about farming at the outset. They developed a mixed farming operation of Jersey and Guernsey milk cows, Leghorn chickens, and a fruit orchard. The farm today is yet owned by the Sussel family.[237]

Nathan J. Tall was a manufacturers' agent with a deep-seated longing for land. In 1947 he went to Aldergrove, B.C. where he operated Tallacres Farm for twenty-one years. This dairy farm, with a completely automated milking system, was a model for its time, attracted study tour groups from Canada and the United States.[238]

Werner Bick left his native Germany in 1938 at age nineteen. Arriving in Chile with his father, they farmed and operated a cheese factory for thirty years. In 1969 the Bicks moved to Aldergrove, B.C. They operate a 62½-acre dairy farm with 125 head of Holstein cows.[239]

There were a number of Jewish poultrymen in the Vancouver

---

236. Bernie Adelberg (son), Vancouver, interview, by the writer, April 17, 1980.
237. *Pioneers, Pedlars,* pp. 51, 53, 126.
238. *Ibid.,* p. 53.
239. *Ibid*

area. George Biely came to British Columbia in 1932 from Chita, Siberia. After attending University of British Columbia (agriculture) he developed and operated Grandview Poultry Farm in Burnaby, B.C. from 1930 to 1960. This was a six-acre hatchery and egg farm with 7,000 Leghorn chickens which supplied the Vancouver market. Hatching eggs were marketed as far away as California. His brother, Professor Jacob Biely, a distinguished researcher, became head of the poultry science department at UBC and a fellow of the Royal Society of Canada.[240]

Ezak Nep, with his father Joseph, came to Winnipeg from Russia about 1910. They had one of the dairy farms in West Kildonan, Manitoba. Ezak later was among the group of Jewish farmers who established the Rosser Colony in Manitoba. Around 1945 he developed the Coast Poultry Farm in South Vancouver on the delta land of the Fraser River. The land was sold about 1955 to make way for a bridge crossing of the river.[241]

Another major producer was Panco Poultry Ltd. in the Newton district of Surrey, B.C. After graduation from agriculture at UBC, this business was developed by Ted Cohen, son of Prince Rupert pioneer M. B. Cohen, and operated by him from the mid-1940s to the mid-1970s.[242]

From the beginning of the twentieth century Jewish farm settlement in Canada showed steady progress and reached its peak at the time of World War I. In 1921 the ICA made a survey of its colonies. In the five principal colonies there were 201 farmers with a total population of 818. These colonies occupied an area of 60,957 acres of which 30,423 were under cultivation. They produced during that year 212,000 bushels of wheat, 111,000 bushels of oats, as well as flax, barley and rye. Adding the smaller settlements supervised by the ICA, the number of farmers was 314 and the total farm population was 1,278.[243] According to the Dominion Government census of 1921 the total number of Jewish farm operators in Canada was 631 and the grand total of the Canadian Jewish farming population was 2,568.[244]

---

240. *Ibid.*, p. 51.
241. Mollie Mellon (sister), interview, by Leonoff, May 8, 1983.
242. *Pioneers, Pedlars*, p. 51.
243. Belkin, pp. 85, 216.
244. *Canada's Jews*, p. 227.

As part of the war effort the Canadian Government called on farmers to produce more wheat and livestock. The ICA endorsed and promoted this policy. More lands were purchased and large herds of cattle were acquired with bank loans. During the war prices were good and some farmers became prosperous. With the end of the war prices dropped sharply. As a result there were many Jewish farmers who were compelled to abandon their land.[245]

The war also gave the Jewish farm parents, long worried about their children's marrying out of the faith, the opportunity to send their daughters to the cities to work in factories. They were followed by their brothers in the factories and the services. Thus the seeds of disintegration were sown amongst the farmers.[246]

Nevertheless, the ICA continued recruiting candidates for settlement. Before the 1930s depression had set in forty new installations were made. The population of the Hirsch colony increased from eighty-two in 1925 to 170 in 1930. The Sonnenfeld population went from ninety-nine to 227. By 1930 the area occupied by the five principal colonies increased to 65,760 acres, with 36,013 under cultivation.[247] The census of 1931 listed 477 Jewish farm operators and 2,188 Jewish farm residents. Seventy-four percent lived in Western Canada, the largest number being in Saskatchewan where one out of six Jews gainfully employed made his living by farming.[248]

In the 1930s drought, successive crop failures, and the fall of farm prices to disaster levels checked further development and almost ruined the farmers in Southern Saskatchewan.[249] In 1930 the local price of wheat dropped to $0.47 a bushel compared to $1.03 received in 1929. The average cost of producing a bushel was $1.00. In addition severe drought, centered in Southern Saskatchewan, set in during the year 1929 through 1937. This was accompanied by plagues of insects. Government authorities encouraged farmers to abandon their land and move northward where they would have to pioneer all over again. As a result, 781 persons left the municipalities where the Hirsch and Sonnenfeld colonies

245. Belkin, pp. 84-85.
246. *Ibid.*, p. 85.
247. *Ibid.*, pp. 166, 216.
248. *Canada's Jews*, pp. 226-227.
249. Belkin, p. 166.

were located. While some Jewish farmers did join the general movement, the five principal colonies remained intact.[250] A 1938 newspaper article stated:

> One of the remarkable facts about Jewish farm life in
> Saskatchewan is that 62% of the present holders of land have
> retained it for 25 years or longer without moving. In the same
> areas, only 16% of the total population have done the same
> thing.[251]

Between 1929 and March 1931 the Canadian Government
promulgated a policy which forced a general suspension of immigration of farming families. This was of short duration for non-
Jews but for the Jews lasted for almost a decade.[252] Soon after the
Nazis took over in Germany in 1933, Fascists and anti-Semites of
all kinds became very active in Canada, and influenced public
opinion. From 1933 through 1948 Canada admitted a paltry 5,000
Jewish refugees, the worst record in the Western World.[253]

Some experienced Jewish farming families did trickle through
from Europe as nationals of various countries. Under the auspices
of the Canadian railways a total of 204 families of 710 persons
arrived. Most settled in land in Ontario, but twenty-seven families
settled in the Western provinces. Thus by 1941 the Jewish farm
operators increased to 545 and the Jewish farm population to
2,486.[254]

World War II took the young people off the farms to serve in
the armed forces and war industries. After the war when the parents got older, they joined their children who were already established in the cities. And with few Jewish women around most of the
young Jewish men who wished to continue farming either had to
remain bachelors or intermarry. And the flow of new immigrant
families who would have settled on farms was severely curtailed
by the depression and war.

---

250. *Ibid.*, pp. 190-191.
251. *Montreal Standard*, December 3, 1938. These figures are confirmed in
    Canada's Jews, pp. 234-237.
252. Belkin, pp. 169-170, 189.
253. This record has been documented in an exhaustive study of the Canadian
    Government immigration policy during this period: Irving Abella and Harold
    Troper, *None is Too Many: Canada and the Jews of Europe 1933-1948*
    (Toronto, 1982), 336 pp.
254. Belkin, pp. 194-199.

After the war the Canadian Government changed its policy and immigration of Jewish people resumed on a greater scale. But by this time farming in Canada had greatly advanced. By 1945 all Jewish farms in Western Canada were completely mechanized.[255] With mechanical equipment the farmer and his wife alone could work areas as large as 1,000 acres. The small farm units had become uneconomical. Acquisition of additional land and the powerful equipment needed to farm it required extensive capital investment. The ICA made several economic studies and concluded that further land settlement in the prairie provinces would be of doubtful wisdom. Rather, they concentrated on specialized projects such as dairy, poultry and fruit farming in Eastern Canada.[256] For the above reasons, as the pioneer farmers died or retired, the western settlements became depopulated. Thus by the 1950s and 1960s the Jewish farm colonies and groups had disintegrated, leaving only a small remnant, or none at all, in the areas of previous settlement.

The dream of a mass Jewish agricultural movement in Canada was never realized. However, the pioneer farmers were important in the history of the Jewish people of Canada. It is clear that Jewish land settlement made a contribution to the growth of the Jewish community in several ways. It attracted many Jewish immigrants, primarily from Eastern Europe. It enabled them to settle on homesteads where otherwise they may have been barred from entering the country. It provided many, some with limited skills, with a profitable occupation. It gave them an opportunity to establish themselves in private enterprise. Jewish farming also served well from a public relations point of view, helping to raise the prestige of the Jewish community throughout Canada.[257]

It is not commonly recognized that Jewish settlers, except for the Mennonites, were the first immigrants from Central and Eastern Europe to settle on farms in Western Canada. Their settlement predates the German, Ukrainian, Doukhobor, Russian, and Hungarian settlements.[258] They showed that not all Jewish immigrants wanted

255. *Ibid.*, p. 203.
256. *Ibid.*
257. *Ibid.*, pp. 85-86.
258. Robert England, *The Colonization of Western Canada: A Study of Contemporary Land Settlement 1896-1934* (London, 1936), pp. 273-274.

to engage in business, industry or the professions. They demonstrated that Jews can be pioneers even if not motivated by national or religious ideals. They proved that Jews, given the incentive and financial resources, can make as good farmers as other ethnic groups.

These pioneer Jews helped to populate the prairie region, and to develop it as an important economic region of Canada and as a bread basket of the world. They were among the very first to make a contribution to the historical development of agriculture in the principal grain belt of Canada. Sons of the pioneers were among the first to attend the newly-opened agricultural colleges on the prairies. They helped to introduce modern farming methods.

Jewish people were at the forefront in the cooperative movement. The depressed grain and cattle prices in the early 1920s put the farmers in difficult economic straits. The ICA had to disburse 624 loans to consolidate the settlements and to place the farmers in a healthy financial position. The government did very little to help the farmers. Speculation in wheat on the Winnipeg Grain Exchange depressed prices even further. The Canadian farmers then decided to help themselves by organizing their own cooperative marketing agencies.[259]

San Francisco-born Aaron Sapiro had gained international repute for his work in organizing the citrus fruit growers of California into marketing cooperatives. The Farmers Union in Canada in 1923 wrote a letter to Sapiro inviting him to visit prairie Canada. He "combined dedicated brilliance with folksy platform appeal . . . to fire the imagination of thousands of farmers who set forth on a millenarian crusade to sign up the neighbors far and wide in a 100 percent contract pool." In Alberta, Saskatchewan and Manitoba, Sapiro sparked the crusade which resulted in the formation of the three prairie wheat pools in 1923-1924.[260]

The ICA urged the Jewish farmers to join the pools. And almost all did so. The pools became important factors in improving and stabilizing prices. Soon wheat prices almost doubled. At the same time cattle prices also increased.[261]

---

259. Belkin, p. 162.
260. J.F.C. Wright, *Saskatchewan: The History of a Province* (Toronto, 1955), pp. 197, 199.
261. Belkin, p. 162.

In 1933 the first World Grain Exhibition was held in Regina. Owing to the energetic work of Isidore Eisenberg and Louis Rosenberg of the ICA staff, the impressive extent of Jewish farming throughout the world was convincingly presented.[262] In Canada the Jewish Colonization Association made the greatest contribution to immigration aid in the country.[263] The long-lived ICA closed its Canadian office in July, 1978.

Many descendants of the pioneer farmers are now prominent Canadians in business, industry, politics, the professions and the arts, making important contributions to the country. Sons and daughters of Jewish pioneers who continue to farm are living testimony to their parents' and grandparents' courage, determination and faith.

---

262. *Ibid.*, p. 191.
263. *Ibid.*, p. 86.

In preparation of this series of articles, the writer was motivated and greatly assisted by interviews, over the years, with about 200 pioneer farmers and their descendants, and visits to most of the colony sites.

Photograph credits: front cover, Bernie Adelberg; p. 3, Ruth Zukor; p. 5, Norman Klenman; p. 7, Ernest Brotman; p. 9, Eli Barish; p. 13, Sam Barish; p. 23, map by Anita Leonoff; p. 27, Jewish Historical Society of Western Canada; p. 31, Ben Barish; pp. 53, 55, Ray (Rosenberg) Braunstein; p. 57, Archie Brotman; p. 59, Morris Pressman; p. 61, Freda (Waterman) Levy; p. 80, Joan Modrall. Photographs by the writer, pp. 11, 25, 29, 33, 49, 51.

William B. Sylvester, son of Cecelia and Frank Sylvester,
Sylvester Feed Company, Victoria, B. C.

OUR CONTRIBUTOR . . .

CYRIL EDEL LEONOFF — Mr. Leonoff is a resident of Vancouver, B.C., a professional engineer, and he is the archivist of The Jewish Historical Society of British Columbia. He was born and educated in Winnipeg, and is the grandson of Wapella pioneer, Edel Brotman. His study was prepared to commemorate the centenary (1884-1984) of Russian-Jewish land settlement in Western Canada.